Common Core

COMMON CORE

National Education Standards and the Threat to Democracy

Nicholas Tampio

Johns Hopkins University Press

Baltimore

© 2018 Johns Hopkins University Press
All rights reserved. Published 2018
Printed in the United States of America on acid-free paper
9 8 7 6 5 4 3 2 1

Johns Hopkins University Press
2715 North Charles Street
Baltimore, Maryland 21218-4363
www.press.jhu.edu

Library of Congress Cataloging-in-Publication Data

Names: Tampio, Nicholas, author.
Title: Common core : national education standards and the threat to democracy /
    Nicholas Tampio.
Description: Baltimore : Johns Hopkins University Press, 2018. | Includes bibliographical
    references and index.
Identifiers: LCCN 2017019813| ISBN 9781421424637 (hardcover : alk. paper) |
    ISBN 1421424630 (hardcover : alk. paper) | ISBN 9781421424644 (electronic) |
    ISBN 1421424649 (electronic)
Subjects: LCSH: Education—Standards—United States. | Education and state—United
    States. | Educational accountability—United States. | Decentralization in government—
    United States. | Central-local government relations—United States. | Democracy—
    United States.
Classification: LCC LB3060.83 .T36 2018 | DDC 379.1/58—dc23
    LC record available at https://lccn.loc.gov/2017019813

A catalog record for this book is available from the British Library.

*Special discounts are available for bulk purchases of this book. For more information,
please contact Special Sales at 410-516-6936 or specialsales@press.jhu.edu.*

Johns Hopkins University Press uses environmentally friendly book materials, including
recycled text paper that is composed of at least 30 percent post-consumer waste,
whenever possible.

To my sons, Giuliano, Luca, Nicola, and Giorgio

Contents

....

Acknowledgments

....

I thank all of the parents, policymakers, educators, editors, journalists, and students with whom I have communicated about education in the past few years. Sigal Ben-Porath, Deborah Brooks, Barry Garelick, Michael Hynes, Andrew F. March, Patrick McGuinn, Amy Perruso, and Charles Tampio read draft chapters of the book. Fordham University awarded me a faculty fellowship in the fall of 2016 to complete the book. Greg Britton, David Goehring, and the outside reviewer have made the argument stronger with their advice and encouragement. I am grateful to everyone working behind the scenes at Johns Hopkins University Press.

My wife, Gina, and I have been talking about the ideas in this book since I wrote my first blog for the *Huffington Post* about the Common Core in 2012. In addition to editing my work, she fills our house with love, healthy food, and books. I want my sons, to whom this book is dedicated, to love to learn, write, speak, ask questions, make art, exercise, serve the community, appreciate nature, and think. My kids, and all kids, deserve an education that cultivates their joy and wonder.

Common Core

....

Do We Need a Common Core?

I n the spring of 2012, my wife, Gina, worried that something had gone wrong in my son's public school kindergarten class. Gina told me that the Montessori-trained teacher was no longer using a play-based curriculum. Instead, she was making the kids sit on the carpet while she lectured to them.

I wrote to other parents in my son's class to ask if they had noticed a change in the classroom. Several parents responded with details about the transformation. Earlier in the school year, the teacher had taught children about famous painters such as Mary Cassatt, Norman Rockwell, or Pablo Picasso. Children would read about the artists, write about them in journals, give presentations to the class describing their lives, and paint in their styles. Or the teacher would introduce students to biology, having them collect acorns in the neighborhood, place them in soil in an aquarium, and, once the saplings had reached a certain height, plant them in the neighborhood while learning about the Kenyan environmental activist Wangari Maathai.

These kinds of hands-on education activities ended with the adoption of the *Treasures* reading program.[1] The teacher now had to use preapproved curricula, assignments, and tests rather than make her own lesson plans or permit students to do free-choice activities. With other parents in the class, I wrote a letter to the principal detailing our concerns and asking her to stop the pilot program.

1

After receiving my letter, the principal invited me to her office. A veteran educator who would retire at the end of the year, she was friendly and forthcoming. She had installed a "peace garden" behind the school and seemed sympathetic to the principles of progressive education. But she told me that the *Treasures* reading program was aligned with the Common Core. What's the Common Core? I asked. She said that it was a set of standards that identified what students should be able to know and do in English Language Arts (ELA) and math by the end of each school year. She said that the standards were internationally benchmarked and would prepare all children for college and careers.

That last claim raised a red flag for me. Our school district had excellent teachers and programs and regularly sent most graduates to college, including some of the most selective in the country. Why would we abandon what had led to our success? And how could any program claim to prepare all children to succeed in college and careers? Without a proven track record, this pitch for the Common Core seemed like what the tailors told the emperor when selling him his new robe.

After my meeting with the principal, I wrote a blog for the *Huffington Post* about my concerns with the Common Core.[2] I argued that in a big, diverse country, we should not permit one organization or group of people to decide the educational mission for nearly all American public schools. We ought to encourage teachers to create lesson plans that interest the students before them, not follow scripted plans aligned to the Common Core standards. Educators should nurture each child's unique talents and interests, not focus on training students to take standardized tests—an activity that people rarely do at selective colleges, creative jobs, or while participating in the life of the community. Like shooting a flare into the sky, I hoped that my essay would draw the attention of other people who saw problems with the Common Core.

Shortly thereafter, I began communicating with people across the country about the Common Core's impact on public education, Catholic schools, and the homeschool community. I exchanged emails with Christel Lane Swasey, a Mormon mother in Utah who helped launch a website where parents could strategize about fighting the Common Core. I met for coffee with Yvonne Gasperino, a mother who manages the Stop Common Core in New York State Facebook page, who told me how the Obama administration used Race to the Top to incentivize states to adopt the Common Core standards. I forged a friendship with Lisa Rudley, a founder of New York State Allies for Public Education (NYSAPE), a group composed primarily of liberal parents and educators concerned about the New York State Regents Reform agenda that includes the Common Core.

Over the next few years, I would give public talks on the Common Core with New York City public school teacher Jia Lee, New York State High School Principal of the Year Carol Burris, New York State Senator George Latimer, New York State Assemblyman Edward Ra, and many other superintendents, principals, educators, and parents. All of us—Republicans, Democrats, and independents; in cities, suburbia, and rural areas; education progressives and education traditionalists—have negotiated our differences to collaborate in stopping the Common Core's transformation of our schools.

Ravitch to the Rescue

The education scholar Diane Ravitch gave parents a boost when she announced her opposition to the Common Core in 2013.[3] Nearly two decades earlier, Ravitch made a strong case for standards in her book, *National Standards in American Education*. Standards, she argued in 1995, were ubiquitous in modern life and guaranteed quality and consistency in hospitals, highways, food labeling, and the like, and it was time that they helped modernize education.[4] In 2010, then US Secretary of Education Arne Duncan met with Ravitch to discuss the Common Core, and he might have assumed that she would see the standards as the culmination of her life's work. Instead, Ravitch became disillusioned with the project of national education standards and criticized the Common Core in articles, books, interviews, blogs, and tweets.

Ravitch argued that political and economic elites had pushed the Common Core standards upon the country in an undemocratic manner. Four private organizations—the Bill & Melinda Gates Foundation, the National Governors Association, the Council for Chief State Schools Officers, and Achieve—had worked behind the scenes with the Obama administration to orchestrate the Common Core State Standards Initiative.[5] At the height of the Great Recession, the Obama administration incentivized states to adopt its education priorities in order to receive a No Child Left Behind (NCLB) waiver or a Race to the Top grant. Though the Obama administration did not require states to adopt the Common Core standards, the federal government did use financial sticks and carrots to pressure states to adopt the standards "with minimum public engagement."[6] For Ravitch, this is not how democracy works, where power must be exercised *by* the people and not just *on* the people.

The architects of the Common Core State Standards Initiative did not follow the international and national protocols for writing standards. According to the American National Standards Institute (ANSI), standards must be "developed in an environment that is equitable, accessible, and responsive to the requirements of various stakeholders."[7] However, the process of writing the Common Core standards took place in secrecy, the writers had to sign confidentiality agreements, and the writing teams included many people from testing organizations such as the College Board and ACT but few experienced teachers or early childhood educators.[8]

This is not just a procedural concern. In 2010, early childhood health and education professionals reviewed the Common Core early-grade standards and warned that they would lead to didactic instruction, an excessive focus on instruction in literacy and math, inappropriate standardized testing, and the crowding out of experiential activities.[9] Those professionals highlighted in particular the kindergarten standard that children "read emergent-reader texts with purpose and understanding" and warned that the resulting emphasis on early literacy would likely harm many children's curiosity and imagination and make them less engaged students or responsible citizens over time. Unfortunately, there is no process to appeal or revise the Common Core standards in light of experience or scholarly critiques.[10]

The people leading the Common Core State Standards Initiative, Ravitch continued, often seem to have ulterior motives. For education reformers such as former Florida governor Jeb Bush, former New York City education chancellor Joel Klein, and former secretary of state Condoleezza Rice, the Common Core tests will provide a "rude awakening" to public school parents that will lead them to support privately managed charter schools and vouchers.[11] For Ravitch and other critics of neoliberal education reform, the Common Core can be a Trojan horse for high-stakes testing, privatization policies, data collection, and corporations seeking a larger share of education budgets.

Finally, Ravitch warned that the new Common Core tests would likely harm many English language learners, students with disabilities, and poor children.[12] Ravitch's warning was borne out when New York started to administer a Common Core-aligned Algebra I Regents examination that many students could not pass. At one New York City high school with a high percentage of recent immigrants, pass rates fell from 63 percent on the previous algebra test to 14 percent on the Common Core test. For Ravitch, the consequence of Common Core testing would be that more students would fail to earn a high school diploma and face a life of diminished economic and civic prospects.[13]

Ravitch remains a prominent critic of the Common Core and the entire project of national education standards.[14] My book adds to Ravitch's work by considering the strongest arguments for and against national education standards; scrutinizing the de facto or proposed national standards in ELA, math, science, honors US history, and sexual health; and envisioning an alternative to national standards in the current political environment.

According to an EdNext opinion poll, public support for the Common Core dropped from 65 percent to 49 percent between 2013 and 2015, while teacher support for the standards during that same period plummeted from 76 percent to 40 percent.[15] It will be interesting to see how the Common Core battle plays out in the next few years, particularly as the Every Student Succeeds Act of 2015 contains provisions that seem to force states to keep the standards while also providing escape routes.[16]

Common Core opponents confront a series of difficult questions. Is the problem the substance of the Common Core standards in ELA and math themselves, or their implementation? If the problem is the standards themselves, is the solution to create better national education standards or to empower states, local education authorities, and/or families to decide education content standards? And how should people view the national education standards on the horizon in science, honors US history, and sex education?

In this book, I argue that large, pluralistic democracies such as the United States should *not* adopt national education standards. My argument is liberal, insofar as I believe in the intrinsic good of diverse ways of living and thinking, and democratic, in that I appreciate the value of ordinary people having a say in the philosophy guiding their local public schools. I acknowledge that there are strong arguments for national education standards in certain times and places and that national education standards can contain many things that young people should probably study in school. To break the theoretical stalemate, I look at real-world debates about specific standards. What we find again and again is that national education standards alienate ordinary citizens from the schools and from political life more generally.[17] In other words, national education standards tend to make our country less rather than more democratic. In the conclusion, I consider how Congress could reconfigure the Elementary and Secondary Education Act (ESEA) to encourage meaningful local education control. In the epilogue, I commend the Common Core test refusal movement for reminding Americans of the importance of democracy as a way of life and not just a way to select leaders every few years.

The Role of Standards

Many debates are ongoing in American education policy, including important ones about equitable funding, early childhood education, teacher training, professional development, class size, technology in the classroom, charter schools, wraparound services, data collection, and higher education. Why focus on standards rather than other pressing education issues? The reason is that standards justify many planks of the education reform movement. Since at least the 1983 publication of the landmark report "A Nation at Risk," reformers have tried to wrestle education policy from progressives working in the tradition of John Dewey.[18] Dewey believed schools should prepare students to express their own unique personality in ways that enrich the community. If a public school has a garden, art classes, theater programs, automobile garages, sports teams, sponsors field trips and internships, or encourages teachers to exercise their own creativity when designing the curriculum, then one sees Dewey's legacy.[19] The education reform movement, by contrast, wants public schools to set and enforce high standards, primarily in literacy and numeracy. Though reformers debate among themselves about pedagogy, educational content, and questions of federalism, they tend to support education standards that pressure educators to impart the skills that workers need to use in the global economy.[20]

In 2010, then US Secretary of Education Arne Duncan explained how standards are the foundation of systemic education reform in "Thinking beyond Silver Bullets," a speech he delivered at the Whole System Reform Conference, in Toronto, Canada.[21] According to Duncan, public schools have been "lying to students and parents" and telling them that students are ready for careers and college when they are not. As evidence, Duncan pointed to America's middling rank on the Program for International Student Assessment (PISA). According to Duncan, the task is to build an education system on the foundation of national education standards:

> In March of 2009, President Obama called on the nation's governors and state education chiefs "to develop standards and assessments that don't simply measure whether students can fill in a bubble on a test, but whether they possess 21st century skills like problem-solving and critical thinking and entrepreneurship and creativity." Virtually everyone thought the president was dreaming. But in six short months, 35 states and the District of Columbia have chosen to adopt the state-crafted Common Core standards in math and English. Additional states are signing on over the next several months. As of today, just over three-fourths of all U.S. public school students now reside in states that have voluntarily adopted higher common, college-ready standards. That is an absolute game-changer in a system which until now set 50 different goalposts for success.[22]

In the rest of his speech, Duncan explained how the Common Core would transform the American education system.

The Common Core provides the basis for a new generation of standardized tests. The No Child Left Behind Act of 2001 required states to test children in ELA and mathematics in grades 3 through 8 and at least once in high school. Still, states had latitude to design their own state standards, make their own tests, determine their own passing scores, choose their own accountability mechanisms, and the like. Now, Duncan explained, the Department of Education has awarded $330 million in grant money to two testing consortia: Partnership for Assessment of Readiness for College and Careers (PARCC) and Smarter Balanced Assessment Consortium (SBAC). As a result of these Common Core standardized tests, "millions of schoolchildren, parents, and teachers will know, for the first time, if students truly are on-track for colleges and careers."[23]

The Common Core justifies the creation of longitudinal data systems to measure student progress over time. Policymakers want to know what factors lead to higher test scores, and longitudinal data systems help them harness the power of big data to determine what factors—such as school fiscal information, teacher credentials, and student coursework—lead to success in higher education and the workplace. The goal, according to Duncan, is to be able to look a second grader in the eye and tell him that he is on track to attend a good college.[24]

The Common Core enables the creation and implementation of a high-stakes testing system. President Obama and Secretary Duncan believe in "incorporating student achievement as one of a number of factors in evaluations of teacher and school performance." In other words, Common Core testing will enable policymakers to identify teachers and schools with high or low student test score growth rates and reward and punish them accordingly.

The Race to the Top framework, Duncan continued, will prompt states to "turn around" the lowest-achieving schools. Policymakers will rank schools based on how the student body performs on Common Core tests. Schools with low scores can try interventions such as extra tutoring or new literacy or numeracy programs. If scores still do not rise, then the district can fire many or all of the employees and turn the schools over to private managers, who will run the school as a charter school.

The Common Core has had an impact on nearly every aspect of education policy. Standards influence pre-kindergarten academic programs and public institutions of higher education that must align their introductory courses so that students do not need remediation. Teacher training programs must prepare future teachers to teach the standards, and in-service professional development must train educators in best practices to improve standardized test scores. Elementary, middle, and high school curricula must align to the standards, and even children's museums and zoos feel pressure to offer programs that claim to teach the standards.[25] We have already begun to see all of these developments with the Common Core, and the process may intensify as the country adopts and implements other national education standards.

In the next few years, Secretary Duncan would tell reporters that opposition to the Common Core comes from right-wing political extremists and parents upset that their children weren't as brilliant as those parents thought.[26] These descriptions do not apply to any education activist that I know. From years of reading blogs, attending rallies, and sharing ideas on social media, I have heard the term "Obamacore" used only by defenders of the Common Core seeking to explain away opposition because of personal animosity to the president. Nor do I think that the anti–Common Core movement will recede during the Trump administration just because a Republican is president and the Every Student Succeeds Act claims to bar the federal government from influencing state education standards. People protest the Common Core, as a rule, because it harms people and institutions that they care about.

In this book I draw upon the democratic tradition of American political thought to give voice to the parents and activists who think that the Common Core has made education and civic life worse. I examine the proposed or de facto national education standards in ELA, mathematics, science, honors US history, and sexual health and show that many people have good reasons to oppose their nationalization. In the conclusion, I make a provisional map for how the United States may encourage healthy educational diversity, and in the epilogue I praise the test refusal movement for reviving America's tradition of participatory democracy.

A Map of the Argument

In the first two chapters, I present the best available arguments for why democracies should and should not adopt national education standards. My goal is to help readers appreciate both sides of the debate and raise questions that demand looking at actual standards to see whether it makes sense to nationalize them or not.

I believe that the theoretical arguments and empirical evidence show that democrats should promote local education control, but we should also consider the concerns of people who advocate national standards.

Chapter 1 presents four arguments for national education standards. The *systemic* argument is that national education standards can lead to coherent policies for curriculum, professional development, accountability mechanisms, and support services. Standards-based education reform can focus energy and purpose and lead to better education outcomes. By using standards, an education system can run like clockwork. The *equity* argument holds that national education standards can lead to better curricular options for children across the country. National education standards can close the opportunity gap between children of different racial and ethnic backgrounds, geographic locations, and family incomes. The *economic* argument holds that national education standards can increase the literacy and numeracy rates of the population, and this amplified human capital will raise a country's gross domestic product. For economists who hold this position, national education standards can improve a country's ranking on international tests and create a well-educated workforce. Finally, the *democratic capacities* argument holds that national education standards can teach young children the skills and dispositions to become active citizens as adults. For democrats who hold this position, national education standards can cultivate personal autonomy that will eventually become public autonomy when the citizenry becomes better educated.

Chapter 2 presents four arguments against national education standards. The American constitution does not enumerate education as a federal power. According to the *danger of factions* argument, no one group of like-minded individuals should have the power to determine the educational direction for the entire country. Instead, because it is so easy to abuse, the power to shape education policy should be dispersed among states, localities, and families. Conversely, the *good of participation* argument maintains that education, and civic life, are better when people participate in running the schools.

When people have a meaningful influence on the local schools' philosophy of education, they tend to become more invested in the school and community affairs in general. For the *entrepreneurial* argument, America's "broken" education system of local education control created many opportunities for young people to participate on debate teams, drama clubs, engineering clubs, and the like. Local education control helps nurture children's creativity, curiosity, and entrepreneurship—talents that helped Americans build the world's largest economy. Finally, social scientists have shown how standards-based reform tends to narrow the curriculum for children in low-income and historically disadvantaged communities. According to the *egalitarian* argument, democrats ought to provide all children, not just children of the wealthy and powerful, with a well-rounded education.

At this stage of the book, I anticipate that many readers will still favor the idea of national education standards. How is it possible to persuade people to change their minds about the Common Core or the idea of national education standards in general? My proposal is to look closely at the details of particular sets of standards and enter the scholarly debates about the standards. My argument is not that everything in every set of standards is bad or worthless. Rather, informed, thoughtful people see enough wrong with each set of standards that there are large, and unnecessary, costs to nationalizing them. There are also benefits to empowering communities to have a meaningful voice in local schools and having a wide array of schools in America: Jesuit, International Baccalaureate, Waldorf, Montessori, progressive, classical, French immersion, vocational, homeschools, and so forth. Schools can always be improved, but the best way to do so, politically and pedagogically, is to empower families and communities.

Chapter 3 discusses the Common Core State Standards for ELA & Literacy in History/Social Studies, Science, and Technical Subjects. Initially, I describe how David Coleman became the architect of the Common Core and a lead writer of the Common Core standards. Next, I show how the first ELA anchor standard provides the foundation for close reading, a method of interpreting texts that demands that readers provide precise evidence to answer questions about a textual passage. I then show how the EngageNY Common Core Curriculum and the SAT, a national college entrance exam, test Common Core close reading. Though there are occasions when people need to provide evidence from a text, the chapter criticizes close reading for stifling student creativity and curiosity. The Common Core presents children few opportunities to share their own thoughts or criticize the material that they are reading. In other words, the Common Core teaches children to follow orders rather than to think for themselves, a disposition that will not prepare them for citizenship. I do not argue that the country should nationalize Deweyan education principles, but I do contend that local education authorities should have the option to adopt a progressive education model that encourages self-directed learning in a supportive community.

Chapter 4 discusses the Common Core Mathematics Standards. The chapter begins by reviewing the math wars in American education and Jason Zimba's role in writing the Common Core math standards. I then explain how the standards conceptualize mathematical understanding and show how the EngageNY Common Core Curriculum and the SAT test understanding using multi-step word problems. I then draw upon expert critics to argue that Common Core's emphasis on understanding may harm students who excel in math but lack the verbal abilities to explain their steps or interpret verbose passages and that Common Core's pacing makes it difficult for students to study calculus in high school and then major in a STEM discipline in college. If a community wants to choose Common Core math, that should be its right, but communities should also have a right to choose a traditional mathematics education with a more established track record.

Chapter 5 begins by describing the origins of the Next Generation Science Standards (NGSS), their relationship to the Common Core, and scientific and engineering practices. To anticipate what the NGSS tests will look like when they are unveiled, I examine the

Programme for International Student Assessment (PISA), which is offered as a model in the National Research Council's *A Framework for K–12 Science Education*. This chapter considers two critiques of the NGSS: it marginalizes aspects of science that do not lend themselves to standardized testing; and its conception of sustainability places too much faith in science and technology, rather than hard political choices, in addressing climate change. The chapter argues that the NGSS can redirect time and money away from other valuable ways to teach science. The *Framework* praises computer simulations and deprecates the use of science kits; in a state such as New York, adoption of the NGSS may result in students having fewer opportunities to do hands-on science. Democracies should cultivate a diverse science educational landscape rather than a monoculture.

Chapter 6 is about the Advanced Placement U.S. History (APUSH) curriculum framework. The chapter begins by explaining the origin of APUSH and its transformation under College Board president David Coleman, the architect of the Common Core. Next, the chapter shows how the APUSH test, which can earn high school students college credit, evaluates historical thinking skills by asking students to perform a close reading of historical documents. I describe the controversy that erupted in Jefferson County, Colorado, when the local school board tried to change the APUSH framework and students and teachers protested. Though I do not share the political leanings of the Jefferson County school board, I agree that the APUSH presents an ideological view of American identity with which many conservative scholars disagree. The College Board's intervention in Jefferson County was as much to protect a copyrighted product as to defend intellectual freedom. In the conclusion, I argue that communities should have a right to decide for themselves how to tell their histories and the College Board should not have a de facto monopoly on college credit–bearing high school history courses.

Chapter 7 covers the National Sexuality Education Standards (NSES). The chapter begins by presenting an overview of the history of sexual health education and the origin of the NSES. I then show

how the standards treat gender identity and how *Tools for Teaching Comprehensive Human Sexuality Education* offers lesson plans to teach the NSES on gender identity. The chapter then considers the fact that many Muslims would disagree with the NSES's conception of homosexuality. Democracies, I think, should not try to inculcate in children views that are fundamentally at odds with those of their parents. Does that mean that schools must not teach students about sexual health? No. Democrats may encourage communities to develop or choose sexual health programs, including but not exclusively those aligned with the NSES. On this topic, as on every one considered in this book, people who advocate national education standards should consider the possibility that their philosophy of education may not prevail. Common decency requires parents to choose from a wide range of educational models for their children.

The conclusion calls for an end to the Common Core experiment and a revival of local education control. The chapter begins by describing how the Elementary and Secondary Education Act and its reauthorizations have been the main lever to move the country in the direction of national education standards. By using the threat of withholding Title I funds, the federal government can pressure states to adopt national education standards and aligned reforms. The chapter argues that the Every Student Succeeds Act gestures toward returning power over standards to the states but that the testing and accountability provisions make it difficult for states to choose standards that differ substantially from the Common Core or the Next Generation Science Standards. Some scholars think that authentic assessments can create a new education paradigm in the Common Core era, but this proposal does not address the concerns of parents who feel alienated from public education. It is time for democracies to entrust communities, teachers, parents, and students to create meaningful education experiences.

In the epilogue, I applaud the test refusal movement for forcing a public debate about national education standards and teaching a generation of people about the value of democracy. The epilogue considers why Michael V. McGill, then superintendent of the Scarsdale,

New York, school district, helped launch the test refusal movement in 2001. To illustrate the diversity of the contemporary opt-out movement, the epilogue shows how Michael Hynes and Lori Koerner, a superintendent and principal, respectively, on Long Island, and Jamaal Bowman, a principal in the Bronx, have encouraged blue-collar and historically disadvantaged communities to fight "the tyranny of standardized testing." At the end, I assert that the problem is not just the Common Core or high-stakes testing: it is the national education standards paradigm. Our country needs to revive the democratic tradition of having communities choose the philosophy of education that undergirds the local schools.

ONE

Arguments for National Education Standards

....

This chapter presents four arguments for national education standards. The goal is to understand why so many constituencies—presidents, governors, legislators, business entrepreneurs, civil rights activists, conservatives, liberals, journalists, scholars, and so forth—have tended to support this idea in the past few decades. Though subsequent chapters criticize the idea and reality of national education standards, I respect the claims that schools should be intelligently organized; that we need to close opportunity gaps between children of different racial, economic, and geographic locations; that we need to prepare graduates to enter the modern workforce; and that we need to inculcate skills and dispositions in children so they can become active citizens as adults. We can persuade people only if we consider their arguments in their strongest forms and explain how our alternative can better help us reach our shared objectives. Here, then, are several of the best arguments for national education standards in academia, policy spheres, and American political culture.

The Systemic Argument
....

One argument for national education standards is that they can make an education system "run like clockwork."[1] An early and influential version of the argument appears in Marshall S. Smith and

Jennifer O'Day's 1990 article, "Systemic School Reform." At the time, Smith was the dean of the Stanford University School of Education and O'Day was a doctoral student at Stanford. Subsequently, Smith and O'Day have advocated, refined, and helped implement systemic school reform. This 1990 article, however, deserves its fame for providing a blueprint for systemic education reform during the Clinton, Bush, Obama, and possibly Trump administrations.[2]

According to Smith and O'Day, the American tradition of local control of education leads to chaos: "The fragmented policy system creates, exacerbates, and prevents the solution of the serious long-term problems in educational content, pedagogy, and support services that have become endemic to the system. Our teachers are badly trained, our curricula are unchallenging, and our schools are inhospitable workplaces." The American education system lacks a "coherent strategy for allocating the resources we do have or for overcoming problems in both quality and quantity when they arise."[3] How a problem is described influences what kind of responses are appropriate.[4] According to Smith and O'Day, systemic education reform is necessary to confront the biggest problem of American education: "uncoordinated energy."[5]

Their response to this situation is to find a way to impose a curricular structure on American education. "All of the energy currently generated and used by the multiple levels and responsible parties of our educational governance system would be wonderful if it were coordinated (even loosely) and focused on a set of coherent, progressive, long-term strategies to achieve challenging common goals and outcomes."[6] Their article outlines "a common vision of what schools should be like" and "a coherent set of policies and practices that encourage and support a challenging and engaging curriculum."[7]

Smith and O'Day envision a national curriculum structure that provides all American children access to a high-quality education.[8] Policymakers should invite experts to "set out the best thinking in the field about the knowledge, processes, and skills students from K–12 need to know." These content standards provide the foundation and the scaffolding of the entire education system. They are "the basic drivers of the instructional guidance system" because they tell everyone what students should know at every stage of their schooling.[9] Smith and O'Day consider the idea that all American students could follow the same curriculum, but they think this approach goes too far in stifling local initiative. In the American context, curriculum frameworks provide an appropriate mix of guidance and flexibility, leaving it up to states and localities to determine how to reach the standards and thus preserve elements of local control. Once the nation has agreed upon content standards, policymakers can bring all of the major elements of the American education system—including teacher hiring, professional development, curriculum, assessment, and accountability mechanisms—into alignment.

Smith and O'Day provide a striking image of what educational governance should look like in a smoothly running education system: a voyage. The state, representing the general public, provides a description of the "ultimate destination of the journey" in the form of curriculum frameworks. Administrators and teachers have "the primary responsibility to chart the course, assemble the necessary provisions and crew, and pilot the ship."[10] Under no condition, however, may people inside the school or district decide the academic destination. That is precisely the problem that systemic education reform seeks to solve: "a chaotic, multi-layered, and fragmented educational governance system in the USA has spawned mediocre and conservative curricula and instruction in our schools."[11]

In the decades following the appearance of this article, Smith, O'Day, and other education reformers have debated among themselves about the content of the curriculum frameworks; whether and how they should be coupled with "opportunity to learn" standards that provide financial resources to provide the materials and personnel required to teach the content standards; the respective roles of the federal, state, and local governments; and whether charter schools or public schools best advance standards-based reform. Reformers tend to agree, however, that local control wastes energy, often provides an inferior education to poor and minority students, ignores the benefits of standardization in multiple areas of modern life, and goes against the trend of the federal government ensuring that all American children have equal educational opportunities. For Smith, O'Day, and their readers, America needs an education system grounded on the same academic standards for all children.

The Equity Argument

Like Marshall S. Smith, Linda Darling-Hammond was a professor in the Graduate School of Education at Stanford University and a member of the Pew Forum on School Reform.[12] In 2008, Darling-Hammond served as director of President Obama's education policy transition team and was a leading candidate to become Hillary Clinton's secretary of education. In 2010, she published her magnum opus, *The Flat World and Education*, which contends that national education standards may help close the "opportunity gap" between children of different economic, racial, and geographic backgrounds.

Darling-Hammond appeals to a certain vision of equality expressed in the Declaration of Independence, the Reconstruction Amendments to the Constitution, *Brown v. Board of Education*, the Elementary and Secondary Education Act, and the election of Obama, an African American, as president of the United States. "The USA is founded on the idea of educational equality. A major part of our national heritage is our collective commitment to the notion that all men and women are 'created equal and entitled to life, liberty, and the pursuit of happiness.' Furthermore, according to the 14th Amendment, all are entitled to equal protection under the law. However, the realization of these ideals has required long struggle, in education and in other arenas of national life."[13] Darling-Hammond's argument is not that the federal government should guarantee equal outcomes to children regardless of race or class; rather, the

American ideal of equity means that all children ought to have an opportunity to make successful lives for themselves.

The major problem in American education, according to Darling-Hammond, is that some students, because of their racial, economic, or geographic backgrounds, face an "opportunity gap" in their educational prospects. Multiple factors contribute to this gap, including poverty, limited early learning opportunities, resegregation, unequal access to qualified teachers, and dysfunctional learning environments. The most serious problem, fortunately, also happens to be the one that is comparatively easy to remedy: lack of access to a high-quality curriculum. "High-quality instruction . . . has been found to matter more for school outcomes than students' backgrounds."[14] If schools provide all children with high-quality curricular materials, then schools are on the way to closing the opportunity gap between white and minority, rich and poor children.

In *The Flat World and Education*, Darling-Hammond looks to high-performing countries such as Finland, Sweden, Korea, Japan, and Hong Kong that "equalize access to a common, intellectually ambitious curriculum."[15] In America, alas, "access to a high-quality curriculum—that is, a combination of ambitious, well-sequenced goals for learning enacted through intellectually challenging assignments, strong instruction, and supportive materials—is relatively rare."[16] If America can provide all children a thinking curriculum, then the country can start to remedy injustices such as the historical legacy of slavery and the persistence of overt and subtle racism.[17]

Darling-Hammond has mixed feelings about the Common Core standards and hopes that they can be used as "guideposts and not straitjackets."[18] In general, however, she supports the idea of national education standards and the role of the federal government and private partners in making them a reality:

As the fate of individuals and nations is increasingly interdependent, the quest for access to an equitable, empowering education for all people has become a critical issue for the

American nation as a whole. As a country, we can and must enter a new era. No society can thrive in a technological, knowledge-based economy by depriving large segments of its population of learning. The path to our mutual well-being is built on educational opportunity. Central to our collective future is the recognition that our capacity to survive and thrive ultimately depends on ensuring to all our people what should be an unquestioned entitlement—a rich and inalienable right to learn.[19]

For Darling-Hammond, the history of American education shows that local control often leads to racist and classist policies. Instead, she thinks that national education standards—and other reforms such as authentic assessment, rigorous teacher training, and multi-faceted accountability mechanisms—may provide all children with an equitable, high-quality education.

The Economic Argument

A remarkable feature of the national education standards movement is that it includes Democrats and Republicans, liberals and conservatives, civil rights activists and business entrepreneurs.[20] To understand what motivates the business community, we may turn to the 2014 report, *Lasting Impact: A Business Leader's Playbook for Supporting America's Schools*, published by the Harvard Business School, the Boston Consulting Group, and the Bill & Melinda Gates Foundation. According to this report, business needs to step up to solve the problem of a shortage of skilled employees. One way to do that is to lay the policy foundations for education innovation, including supporting the Common Core and Next Generation Science Standards.

According to the report, American students do not have the intellectual capital to succeed in the global economy. The report points to America's scores on the Program for International Student

Assessment (PISA), a standardized test of 15-year-olds in literacy, numeracy, and science administered every three years by the Organisation for Economic Co-operation and Development (OECD). In 2012, nineteen of sixty-five countries scored higher than the United States in reading and twenty-nine scored higher in mathematics. Citing the research of Stanford University economist Eric Hanushek, the report warns that low PISA scores suggest that a country's growth in gross domestic product will plateau or not grow as rapidly: "A country short of accomplished students today will be starved of talent, innovation, and growth tomorrow."[21]

The report says that the business community has been mistakenly playing a short game rather than a long one. Business leaders "write checks, donate computers, sponsor student scholarships, encourage employees to volunteer time, and take other steps with immediate effect—but with little enduring, systemic impact."[22] It is not solely a moral question of helping the least advantaged: businesses have a financial incentive to fix the schools. "Well-educated students become skilled and productive employees, and prosperous employees become avid consumers. Compared to high-school dropouts, graduates pay more taxes, draw less from social welfare programs, and are less likely to commit crimes."[23]

The most urgent need is for the business community to rally to the cause of national education standards in literacy, numeracy, and science. "Business has been a strong supporter of college- and career-ready standards. By highlighting America's need for a talent pool at least equal to that of other countries, business leaders have helped make the case for the adoption of new standards." The report lists activities that business leaders can undertake to support the Common Core State Standards and the Next Generation Science Standards. For example, they can publicly announce their support for the standards at the national, state, and local level; write to and meet with governors and state legislators; fund different components of standards-based reform such as professional development programs; prepare the public for the backlash that may arise with initial lower test scores; and "educate and enlist employees as supporters."[24]

In recent years, conservative activists have challenged the business community for supporting the Common Core. Though some business leaders have backed away from the Common Core's "toxic brand," many remain committed to the notion that national education standards are essential to prepare a country's workforce to succeed in the global economy.[25] In addition, some civil rights activists are sympathetic to the argument that schools should focus on teaching minority and poor students the skills they need to get and hold a good-paying job.[26]

The Democratic Capacities Argument

It is possible that a country's education program can be systematic and equitable while preparing children for the modern economy— and still not be democratic. For those who cherish the democratic ideal of government by, for, and of the people, are national education standards a good idea? Yes, according to professors Benjamin I. Bindewald (Oklahoma State), Rory P. Tannebaum (Merrimack College), and Patrick Womac (University of Maine) in their 2016 article, "The Common Core and Democratic Education." Their argument is that national education standards, and the Common Core in particular, "help young citizens develop knowledge, skills, and dispositions required for active participation in a pluralist, democratic society."[27]

According to Bindewald, Tannebaum, and Womac, schools in a democracy need to teach children how to exercise private and public autonomy. Private autonomy is an "opportunity and capacity to think for oneself, to set one's own goals, and to pursue those goals free from excessive outside influence."[28] Private autonomy also includes the ability to choose one's own job, move around the country, choose one's religion, and think and reflect on important social issues. It reflects Kant's principle that we should have the courage to use our own understanding in deciding how we live our own lives. Liberal democrats value private autonomy when they consider the alternative: educational arrangements that teach children to respect only people of the same religion, scientific curricula that deny the truth of evolution, or families that do not teach children how to read.

Public autonomy is "a community's opportunity and capacity to influence public life and shape public policy"; it is the capacity for people to perform their role as citizens working together on matters of the common good.[29] Public autonomy is the ability to run for public office or participate in a civil political debate. Ideally, public schools should inculcate public autonomy as well as private autonomy, but, the authors trust, private autonomy tends to lead to public autonomy. For instance, if you learn how to keep an open mind about one's religious commitments, you will tend to tolerate people of other religions and want to work together on political projects.

According to these criteria, the authors contend that the Common Core ELA standards do an excellent job teaching children private autonomy and only a fair job teaching public autonomy. The authors note that the standards "set higher benchmarks encouraging students to actively participate in processes that require the use of higher order thinking. They aim to develop students who habitually perform the critical reading and thinking necessary to carefully navigate the staggering amount of information available to learners in the 21st century. They also direct students to consider multiple perspectives, engage in a process of evaluating these perspectives according to multiple sources of evidence, and examine how biases (including their own) influence this process."[30] The authors wish that the standards placed more emphasis on democratic citizenship, but they argue that the standards do teach, for example, critical thinking skills that are essential to healthy democratic politics. By learning how to examine multiple perspectives in a passage, students are subtly learning the skills of deliberation that they may exercise when serving, for example, on a city council.

The authors consider the objection that the Common Core leads to a loss of local control but dismiss it because standards are not curriculum and localities have some discretion about how to teach the standards. But even if a community loses some opportunity to influence what happens in the schools, this loss is outweighed by the "capacity components of public autonomy."[31] In other words, the Common Core teaches children how to exercise public autonomy when they become adults. A democracy should not risk educating the next generation of citizens just because the locals have bad ideas about how to teach literacy and numeracy.[32]

Conclusion

In this chapter, I have presented several of the strongest arguments that I can find to justify national education standards. I have quoted authors extensively to make sure that I am not misrepresenting their positions and so that readers have leads if they want to learn more about the arguments. In chapter 2, I present the best theoretical arguments I can find against national education standards, and in chapters 3–7, I show that there is a disconnect between the claims made on behalf of national education standards and what happens when they are implemented in democratic, pluralistic societies.

But I think that each of the arguments discussed in this chapter contains a grain of truth. Schools need the help of experts to coordinate different aspects of an education system. Democracies should work to ensure that all children get a quality education. Schools should impart the skills that children need to work in the modern world. And public education should prepare children to become democratic citizens.

TWO

Arguments against National Education Standards

....

This chapter presents four arguments against national education standards: National education standards empower one group of like-minded people, or faction, to impose their pedagogical views on the entire country. They alienate ordinary citizens from the local schools and civic life in general. They crowd out special activities that often cultivate student creativity and entrepreneurship. And they narrow the curricular options for students in poor and historically disadvantaged communities.

The previous chapter and this one reprise a debate that has run throughout American history between those who want to centralize power, such as the Federalists, and those who favor dispersed power, such as the Democratic Republicans. National education standards express the Hamiltonian impulse to invest power in a single set of experts, usually but not necessarily in the federal government. The argument against national education standards, in turn, hinges on the Jeffersonian-Madisonian view that democracy requires communities to have meaningful freedom over the schools.[1] In chapters 3–7, I argue that the devil-in-the-details of the de facto or proposed national education standards may make democrats here and now favor decentralized education control.

The US Constitution does not enumerate education as one of the federal government's powers. Why not? We can answer this question by looking to the Federalist Papers. Written during the ratification debates in 1787 and 1788, they explain how the Constitution will rectify the problems of the Articles of Confederation without placing too much power in the capital. Though Publius was the pseudonym for the author of the Federalist Papers, the two most important writers, the New York lawyer Alexander Hamilton and the Virginia politician James Madison, disagreed on how to distribute power among the federal government, the states, and the executive and the legislative branches. Hamilton wanted the federal government and executive branch to be strong so that America could compete on the global stage, while Madison valued states' rights and placing checks on federal power. In this section, I offer a Madisonian explanation for why national education standards risk tyranny by granting too much power to a single faction.

In his contributions to the Federalist Papers, Madison explains why the Constitution divides and separates powers when things would run more smoothly, it seems, if power were more clearly and centrally located. Throughout history, republics have ended because of civil war between factions. "By a faction, I understand a number of citizens, whether amounting to a majority or a minority of the whole, who are united and actuated by some common impulse of passion, or of interest, adverse to the rights of other citizens, or to the permanent and aggregate interests of the community." According to Madison, the "causes of faction are sown in the nature of man" and manifest themselves in "a zeal for different opinions concerning religion, concerning government, and many other points." In a free society, people will tend to congregate with friends, family members, coreligionists, and people with a similar political ideology, and they will tend to disagree with people of other religions, classes, locales, and so forth. "As long as the reason of man continues fallible, and he is at liberty to exercise it, different opinions will be formed."[2] Madison thinks that all human beings belong to factions, and any one faction's conception of the good may look like a mischievous plan to the others. In other words, Madison does not grant any one faction the right to speak for the public good.

Throughout history, republics have tried to stop civil war by eliminating factions, an attempt which, according to Madison, has led to violence, resentment, and the death of republics. If republics are free, then people will form factions, and proposing to save a republic by eliminating liberty is a cure worse than the disease.[3]

Madison's genius idea in the Federalist Papers is that a republic may survive if many factions have power. Ancient republics ended in war because one faction or another tried to decimate the opposition. A modern republic may survive, however, if the constitutional structure prevents any one faction, even one that includes a majority of citizens, from ruling just as it wishes. That is the advantage of America's size and diversity: "Extend the sphere, and you take in a greater variety of parties and interests; you make it less probable that a majority of the whole will have a common motive to invade the rights of other citizens; or if such a common motive exists, it will be more difficult for all who feel it to discover their own strength, and to act in unison with each other."[4] For Madison, the Constitution entrusts the federal government to protect "the great and aggregate interests" and the states and localities to handle the rest.[5] The Constitutional structure permits factions to congregate in certain parts of the country and live in ways unpalatable to people elsewhere.

More pointedly, the Constitution gives local and state politicians tools and weapons to fend off federal power. "The great security against a gradual concentration of the several powers in the same department, consists in giving to those who administer each department the necessary constitutional means and personal motives to resist the encroachments of others. . . . Ambition must be made to counteract ambition."[6] Madison's wager is that a low-simmering civil war will better preserve a republic than trying to end strife between factions once and for all. The Founders designed the Constitution with a complicated system of checks and balances, a messy allocation of executive power to three levels of government, and a Bill of Rights that permits citizens to criticize and assemble to petition the government in order to make it difficult for any one faction to oppress the others. Throughout American history, politicians have bewailed the inefficiency of the constitutional framework and the difficulty of making large-scale public policies. It bears repeating: the Constitution was designed to place roadblocks in the way of factions tyrannizing other factions.

In *An Education in Politics: The Origins and Evolution of No Child Left Behind*, the political scientist Jesse H. Rhodes identifies five factions in American education policy debates:

- Business entrepreneurs such as Louis Gerstner of IBM and Ed Rust of State Farm who advocate federal involvement in education and believe in the standards, testing, and accountability paradigm

- Civil rights entrepreneurs such as Kati Haycock, of Education Trust, and Marshall Smith, undersecretary of education during the Clinton administration, who agree with business entrepreneurs about the aforementioned points but want the federal government to equalize education spending

- Educational liberals such as Monty Neill, of FairTest, and National Education Association president Mary Futrell, who support federal education spending but oppose the standards, testing, and accountability paradigm from a Deweyan perspective

- Educational conservatives such as Chester E. Finn Jr., of the Thomas B. Fordham Institute, and Senator Lamar Alexander (R-TN), who prefer a smaller federal footprint in education but want states and localities to work within the standards, testing, and accountability paradigm

- State officials such as then Governors Bill Clinton and George W. Bush, who tend to agree with education conservatives but sometimes are less enthusiastic about vouchers and charter schools[7]

Furthermore, as we will see in this book, well-educated, thoughtful people disagree profoundly about how to teach literacy, learn mathematics, introduce children to science, teach honors US history, and frame questions of gender identity. There are many political and pedagogical factions in the standards debate.

From a Madisonian perspective, people in a free society tend to disagree about how to educate children. A free society ought to create space for many factions to shape education—on the condition that people can exit to other educational models if they so choose. People who favor national education standards may have to use deceit, threats, or force to secure the acquiescence of all Americans. At the end of the book, I argue that the test refusal movement shows that many citizens become angry, rightfully, when certain factions try to impose their educational vision on the entire country.[8]

The Good of Participation Argument

The first argument is primarily negative: national education standards are a tool whereby one faction may dictate how other people educate their children. But one can also argue, positively, that empowering communities to run the schools enriches civic life and education. This is Alexis de Tocqueville's thesis in *Democracy in America*.

Tocqueville was a French aristocrat who visited America in 1831–1832 and then published *Democracy in America*, "at once the best book ever written on democracy and the best book ever written on America."[9] Tocqueville argued that America's founding as a country without a feudal past came with a price: individualism. In a feudal society, people know their distant ancestors and feel a bond to their great-grandchildren. In a feudal society, people feel warmth for people above and below them and know their place within a community. In America, however, there are no aristocrats or serfs, and people retreat to the small circle of friends and family that they already know. Tocqueville calls this tendency to shrink the size of one's social circle individualism—"a reflective and peaceable sentiment that disposes each citizen to isolate himself from the mass of those like him and to withdraw to one side with his family and his friends."[10] Individualism tends to make people care about fewer and fewer people and eventually become indifferent to most other people and society at large. Think of gated suburban communities where people rarely talk with their neighbors or strangers.

Fortunately, Tocqueville argues, Americans have found the remedy for individualism: free institutions. "Americans of all ages, all conditions, all minds constantly unite. . . . Everywhere that, at the head of a new undertaking, you see the government in France and a great lord in England, count on it that you will perceive an association in the United States."[11] In America, ordinary people build hospitals, raise churches, and found and maintain schools. Part of what makes democracy in America work, according to Tocqueville, is that many people participate in governing the community.

Democracy in America explains how civic participation ennobles and enlarges the worldview of ordinary people. "When citizens are forced to be occupied with public affairs, they are necessarily drawn from the midst of their individual interests, and from time to time, torn away from the sight of themselves." "By charging citizens with the administration of small affairs . . . one interests them in the public good and makes them see the need they constantly have for one another in order to produce it." "The free institutions that the inhabitants of the United States possess and the political rights of which they make so much use recall to each citizen constantly and in a thousand ways that he lives in society."[12] For Tocqueville, people become fit to rule by ruling. People discover and cultivate abilities they don't even know they have before they perform civic roles in the community.

In Tocqueville's eyes, American democracy creates a virtuous circle in which free institutions and energetic citizens reinforce each other. Free institutions give people opportunities to make public speeches, research political issues, talk to neighbors, read and write for newspapers, and think about things outside of their home and neighborhood. At the same time, an energetic citizenry tends to improve the quality of the schools, hospitals, churches, and the like. Parents make schools better when they join parent-teacher associations, accompany students on field trips, run for school board, fundraise, make or choose standards, deliberate about and decide curricula, consult experts, and hold schools accountable by voting for budgets and school board members.

Jesse H. Rhodes presents empirical evidence to support Tocqueville's argument in his 2015 *Political Behavior* article, "Learning Citizenship? How State Education Reforms Affect Parents' Political Attitudes and Behavior." Rhodes collected data on states' education policies and administered an original survey for public school parents. After running a regression, he discovered that "parents residing in states with more developed assessment systems express significantly lower trust in government, substantially decreased confidence in government efficacy, and much more negative attitudes about their children's schools." Top-down education reforms alienate parents from the schools and civic life in general. "These policies demobilize parents by excluding them from key educational decisions and enmeshing their children's schools in a punitive testing context that elicits parental anxiety and dissatisfaction."[13] One sometimes hears the argument that top-down education reform better prepares children *for* democracy even if they do not necessarily receive an education *in* democracy.[14] Rhodes challenges that view by citing scholarship showing that "parental support for and involvement in education are essential both to student achievement and to broader school success."[15]

For Tocqueville, America's tradition of local control energizes parents and community and makes school a valued civic institution. Discarding this tradition risks opening the door to individualism.

Rhodes brings this argument into the present. If parents cannot meaningfully influence the local school's philosophy of education, then they are less inclined to run for school board, attend PTA meetings, or participate in community affairs. This lack of participation is not good for students, and it is not good for democracy.[16]

The Entrepreneurial Argument

One of the main arguments for national education standards is that they can, if bundled with aligned reforms, improve a country's economic standing, but a prominent opponent of this view, Yong Zhao, believes that local education control creates more opportunities for young people to develop their entrepreneurial capacities than a system predicated on standardization.

Yong Zhao was born in the Sichuan province in China and received a bachelor's degree from Sichuan Institute in Chongqing. He earned his doctorate at the University of Illinois and is presently Foundation Distinguished Professor in the School of Education at the University of Kansas. In *World Class Learners*, Zhao addresses the fact that China and other East Asian countries regularly rank among the top on the PISA international standardized test. The reason for this success, Zhao explains, is that the Chinese education system is geared toward preparing students for the *gaokao* college entrance exam, itself a reincarnation of the thousand-year-old *keju* exam to become a government official. "The *keju* has ingrained in the Chinese psyche that book knowledge is the only way to gain social and economic status—the only way to enter the ruling class."[17] Based on test scores alone, it appears that East Asian countries have the best education system in the world—which may be one reason that former US Secretary of Education Arne Duncan held them up as a model for American education reform efforts.[18]

In *World Class Learners*, however, Zhao warns Americans that the Chinese education system crushes the creativity and entrepreneurship of its young people. In China, parents want children to maintain a laser focus on preparing for the *gaokao* and ignore all of their other interests and talents. "With an absence of opportunity for exploration and experimentation, the creative and entrepreneurial potential remains dormant at the best, and withers at the worst."[19] Students who show talent in the arts, business, or sports are often sorted out of an academic system that prizes test scores above all. Students who remain in the system lose creativity and curiosity, because they are penalized whenever they think outside the box. Children spend little time socializing with their friends, and their passions wither like a plant that is rarely watered. Children lose confidence in themselves, and when they finally do get to college they often just go through the motions. For Zhao, it is telling that China, given its size, has so few Nobel Prize winners, globally famous artists, or utility patents; it is also telling that farsighted Chinese education policymakers look to America for insights on how to nurture skills in young people that lead to inventions and start-up companies.[20]

In *World Class Learners*, Zhao identifies several features of American education, primarily before No Child Left Behind, that have contributed to the country's having the largest economy in the world. For instance, Americans have not been obsessed with preparing for standardized tests in core academic subjects. At the same time, American students have been free to pursue their passions, such as music, sports, glass blowing, debate teams, theater programs, engineering club, math Olympiad, and other extracurricular activities. The American education system does not coordinate the curricula, assessments, teacher training, and so forth. Rather, local autonomy "gives teachers and the schools the freedom to develop programs and activities that are potentially more relevant to their students."[21] Compared to their international peers, American children have more time and opportunity to go out for sports teams, prepare for talent shows, or join orchestras. American children have more time to socialize, manage relationships, and be responsible and independent. They are happier, more confident students who are willing to take risks on becoming pop stars, novelists, or entrepreneurs.

Zhao thinks that we should celebrate the good features of American education and avoid the sky-is-falling rhetoric pervasive in education reform literature since the 1983 report, "A Nation at Risk."

For Zhao, America ought to go further in the direction of an entrepreneur-oriented education paradigm. This paradigm encourages children to pursue their own interests and passions, with teachers helping students find their own path. Instead, America is now embracing an employee-oriented paradigm that "requires an apparatus with clearly defined learning outcomes for all students."[22] This system may be effective at teaching children a predetermined, static skill set, but it will not help them prepare for many jobs that require imagination, creativity, or boldness. That is why Zhao calls upon Americans to "stop prescribing and imposing on children a narrow set of content through common curriculum standards and testing" and "start personalizing education to support the development of unique, creative, and entrepreneurial talents."[23]

In *World Class Learners*, Zhao quotes the Chinese proverb: "All medicine is poisonous." Zhao knows why people support the US Common Core, the Australian Curriculum, and England's National Curriculum. But he also thinks that this medicine for low scores on international tests will come at the cost of making many bright, creative, energetic kids hate school and lose their entrepreneurial spark.

My primary arguments against national education standards are democratic rather than economic. Like Tocqueville, John Dewey, and Deborah Meier, I oppose education centralization and standardization because they harm the democratic fiber of our schools and our country.[24] Still, Zhao provides a counterpoint to the systemic and economic arguments for national education standards that we considered in chapter 1. America's "broken" education system of local control led to our generating the world's largest economy. Americans ought to be wary of fixing the system by removing the elements that help all children, of whatever income and race, develop the talents that our country needs to compete in the twenty-first-century global economy.

The Egalitarian Argument

According to the political scientist Jesse H. Rhodes, the main alliance that has made possible national education standards is that between business groups and civil rights organizations for standards and accountability (CROSAs). Business entrepreneurs funded organizations such as Achieve, which coordinated the Common Core State Standards Initiative and mobilized support among Republicans. CROSA brought Democrats into the education reform camp and presented national education standards as the natural progression of the federal government's advocating for the poor and historically disadvantaged.[25] There are, however, scholars and activists who contend that egalitarians ought to oppose national education standards, at least the ones on hand, for narrowing the curriculum and life prospects for children in poverty and children of color.[26]

In "From Dewey to No Child Left Behind," researchers then at the University of Texas at Austin—Julian Vasquez Heilig, Heather Cole, and Angélica Aguilar—give two reasons that all children should study the arts. Arts education teaches children to express their thoughts and feelings and appreciate the perspectives of other people, and it also teaches children the democratic virtues of self-assertion and respect for others. Referring to Dewey, they argue that "arts are indeed experience, and that access to arts education opens processes of inquiry that expand a child's perception of the world and create venues for understanding and action."[27] In addition, arts education teaches children, often indirectly, skills that translate into career opportunities. "The benefits of creative initiative may not be as clear and measureable as core subject test scores, but we should not underestimate the value of arts education for our youth."[28] At a commencement address at Stanford University, Steve Jobs remarked that a calligraphy class gave him ideas, a decade later, for how to design the first Macintosh computer—evidence that arts education pays, as it were.

Vasquez Heilig, Cole, and Aguilar describe how Texas education reforms, brought to a national scale when Governor George W. Bush became president, have marginalized art courses in public schools. The No Child Left Behind Act of 2001 and Texas-specific laws and policies focus on students mastering the standards in math, science, and literacy. High-stakes tests make teachers and administrators focus above all on students testing well on the material—or people lose their jobs.[29] Nearly all public schools have increased instructional time in the tested subjects, but the focus on test-taking strategies is even greater in lower-performing schools populated by low-income students and students of color.[30] "Our education system is founded on notions of equity and opportunity. The arts are a fundamental equalizer, but not when their study is systematically denied. Policymakers, educators, and other stakeholders need to understand the arts' intrinsic value and the way they allow students to view the world in a new way, open up perspectives through alternative means of expression, engage the senses, and, above all else, provide access to knowledge through appreciation of the aesthetic experience."[31]

One objection may be that it makes little sense to teach children painting if they don't know how to read and do math well. Given financial limitation, maybe Title I schools should concentrate on teaching basic skills that children will need to get a decent job and entry into college.

Yohuru Williams, dean of the College of Arts and Sciences at the University of St. Thomas, responds to that point in a *Huffington Post* blog post called "Rhythm and Bruise." Williams argues that in the recent past it would have been difficult "to drive through any community without passing one of the gigantic, student-created displays for the local middle school play or attending some parade or festival unaccompanied by the pulsating rhythms of the high school band." These events can teach children twenty-first-century skills such as teamwork, initiative, and perseverance. "From set design and orchestration, to staging and improvisation, music, drama, and art are a collective smorgasbord of practical application." More than that, art displays, theater performances, and marching bands are "meaningful exhibitions of knowledge and the application of acquired skills taking place where everyone can see and enjoy them in public spaces." The arts let children express their individuality in ways that enrich the community.[32] Children in inner-city Detroit and Chicago should be introduced to the arts just as surely as students in the neighboring suburbs. The arts are essential to democratic education and should not be sacrificed in the era of national education standards.[33]

Conclusion

This chapter has laid the theoretical foundation for claims that I make in the rest of the book. One faction made the country's ELA, mathematics, science, honors US history, and sexuality education standards and, as Madison would have predicted, other factions are furious that they have little chance to influence education policy and practice in any meaningful way. The national education standards movement has disempowered communities, marginalized school boards, and alienated people from the local schools. Standards-based reform has brought the country closer to a national education system, but the new system has displaced programs, courses, and extracurriculars that nurture children's talents and interests. And national education standards have financial and opportunity costs that disproportionately affect poor and minority communities. As Plato notes in the *Phaedrus*, inventors tend to anticipate only the positive consequences of their inventions; in the next few chapters, we'll show how the extant national education standards cause problems that their advocates may not want to see.

THREE

English Standards, Close Reading, and Testing

....

This chapter discusses the Common Core State Standards for English Language Arts & Literacy in History / Social Studies, Science, and Technical Subjects. It focuses on the first College and Career Readiness anchor standard that requires students to "read closely to determine what the text says explicitly and to make logical inferences from it" and "cite specific textual evidence when writing or speaking to support conclusions drawn from the text."[1] The first ELA anchor standard lays the foundation for Common Core close reading and influences the Next Generation Science Standards conception of practices and the Advanced Placement U.S. History curriculum framework's notion of historical thinking skills. It also shapes college entrance exams such as the SAT and ACT and whether pre-kindergarten, vocational programs, extracurricular activities, or college courses align to the Common Core. Much of the Common Core debate is about whether the country should nationalize the first ELA anchor standard and its pedagogy of close reading.

I begin this chapter by describing David Coleman's role as architect of the Common Core, lead writer of the ELA standards, and College Board president. Next, I explain his philosophical justification for close reading in his essay, "Cultivating Wonder." Third, I show how the EngageNY Common Core Curriculum and the College Board's redesigned SAT impart and assess student mastery of close reading. The Common Core's expectation that students use exact evidence—and only exact evidence—from the text lends itself to test preparation strategies and computer-based teaching and testing. I then discuss how John Dewey and contemporary progressive educators contest this kind of pedagogy for teaching children to follow directions rather than exercise personal or collective autonomy. In conclusion, I argue that local education authorities should be free to adopt or choose an alternative to the Common Core ELA standards.

The History of the Common Core ELA Standards

On April 28, 2011, the New York State Education Department hosted an event in Albany called "Bringing the Common Core to Life." The main participants were then Commissioner of Education David Steiner and Student Achievement Partners founder David Coleman. In his opening remarks, Steiner said, "When the history of this period is written, I am convinced that David Coleman will be at the very center of the account of educational reform in this country."[2] Coleman has played at least four roles in writing and advocating the Common Core standards.

In 2008, Coleman and Gene Wilhoit, director of the Council of Chief State School Officers (CCSSO), convinced Bill and Melinda Gates to fund and coordinate the Common Core State Standards Initiative. Gates's support was crucial for writing the standards, gaining the endorsements of constituencies such as teachers unions and think tanks, helping states submit Race to the Top applications, and placing Common Core advocates in key positions in the US Department of Education.[3]

In 2009 and 2010, Coleman was a lead writer of the Common Core ELA standards.[4] He used Achieve's earlier effort to create national education standards—the American Diploma Project—as a starting point and consulted with members of the Common Core work groups, feedback groups, and validation groups. There were also opportunities for the public and state education department officials to comment on drafts of the standards. But Coleman is widely considered to be the architect of the Common Core and the main author of the ELA standards.

In 2012 and 2013, Coleman published several documents to explain his philosophy of education and vision of what the Common Core ELA anchor standards mean for teaching and learning. These documents include "Cultivating Wonder," "A Close Reading of Lincoln's Gettysburg Address: A Common Core Unit," and "Revised Publishers' Criteria for the Common Core State Standards in English Language Arts and Literacy, Grades 3–12" (co-authored with Susan Pimentel).

After becoming president and chief executive officer at the College Board in 2012, Coleman aligned the SAT and Advanced Placement courses with the Common Core. The group that Coleman founded, Student Achievement Partners, also partnered with the New York State Education Department to make the EngageNY Common Core Curriculum.

The Philosophy of the Common Core ELA Standards

In his essay, "Cultivating Wonder," published by the College Board in 2013, Coleman explains the philosophy of education that undergirds close reading.

Many students, the essay begins, do not graduate from high school ready for college or careers, but the new standards promise to tear down the wall between students and complex texts. "The Common Core State Standards challenge students to read like a detective and write like an investigative reporter."[5] The Common Core teaches children how to read texts such as manuals so they're ready to enter the workforce. But the Common Core also promises to inculcate a wonder and reverence for texts that will give all students a liberal arts education.[6]

The essay quotes the opening scene in Shakespeare's *Hamlet,* where two security guards change places. Coleman asks us to determine in what tone of voice Bernardo asks, "Who's there?" and he also asks us how we know. "The words that open *Hamlet* are remarkably simple. The challenge is to pay attention. The only source of insight can be the words themselves."[7] To answer the question, we must be able to cite the exact lines that show that Bernardo is spooked.

The first anchor standard remains "in play throughout each of the reading standards that follows. Standard 1 focuses on the command of evidence in what is read, and students must continue [to] draw on evidence as they examine the ideas, structure or style of any text."[8] All of the other anchor standards build upon the first.

The second anchor standard demands that students "determine central ideas or themes of the text and analyze their development" and "summarize the key supporting details and ideas." It requires students to provide evidence from a text to determine the central ideas or theme. Coleman asks how the idea of practice unfolds in an excerpt from Martha Graham's essay, "An Athlete of God." In the first paragraph, Graham says that to practice means to do so "in the face of all obstacles," and in the third paragraph, she explains that "there are daily small deaths." Students should be able to identify this kind of evidence to answer questions about the central ideas or themes of a text.

The third anchor standard requires students to "analyze how and why individuals, events, or ideas develop and interact over the course of a text." To illustrate this standard, Coleman asks about the role of Tom Sawyer in the first chapter of *Adventures of Huckleberry Finn*. To answer this question, Coleman points to the first two paragraphs and the last line of the chapter to see how Tom moves from partner-in-crime to rescuer. "In order to witness Tom's force in the first chapter, we need to pay attention to structure and how the text unfolds."[9]

The remaining anchor standards require students to provide textual evidence to answer questions about words and phrases (4), structure (5), point of view (6), content in diverse media and formats (7), reasoning (8), and similarities to another text (9).[10] So anchor standards 1–3 require students to identify key ideas and

Grade	Standard
K	With prompting and support, ask and answer questions about key details in a text
1	Ask and answer questions about key details in a text
2	Ask and answer such questions as who, what, where, when, why, and how to demonstrate understanding of key details in a text
3	Ask and answer questions to demonstrate understanding of a text, referring explicitly to the text as the basis for the answers
4	Refer to details and examples in a text when explaining what the text says explicitly and when drawing inferences from the text
5	Quote accurately from a text when explaining what the text says explicitly and when drawing inferences from the text
6	Cite textual evidence to support analysis of what the text says explicitly as well as inferences drawn from the text
7	Cite several pieces of textual evidence to support analysis of what the text says explicitly as well as inferences drawn from the text
8	Cite the textual evidence that most strongly supports an analysis of what the text says explicitly as well as inferences drawn from the text
9–10	Cite strong and thorough textual evidence to support analysis of what the text says explicitly as well as inferences drawn from the text
11–12	Cite strong and thorough textual evidence to support analysis of what the text says explicitly as well as inferences drawn from the text, including determining where the text leaves matters uncertain

Source: "Common Core State Standards English Language Arts"

details in a text; anchor standards 4–6 demand that students analyze a text's craft and structure; and anchor standards 7–9 require students to integrate knowledge and ideas about a text. The foundation of the Common Core ELA standards, throughout, is the first anchor standard's demand that students "quote accurately" when answering questions about the passage.

The first Common Core anchor standard increases in intensity as students progress from kindergarten to high school graduation. The basic idea remains that students must be able to provide verbatim evidence from a text when answering questions about it (table 3.1).

Coleman concludes his essay with principles for writing assessment questions. "Great questions make the text the star of the classroom," for "the most powerful evidence and insight for answering lies within the text or texts being read. Most good questions are text dependent and text specific. They reflect a love or reverence for the text at hand."[11]

Coleman's philosophy of education is that students should be able to read any passage of text and answer questions about it by providing text-dependent and text-specific answers. Why? To get a job, but also because "great questions provoke a sense of mystery and provide a payoff in insight that makes the work of reading carefully worth it."[12]

Coleman concludes by noting that close reading can apply to literature and nonliterary fiction but also to social studies, history, science, and technical subjects.[13] In subsequent chapters, I show how close reading permeates the Common Core mathematics standards, the Next Generation Science Standards, the AP US History curriculum framework, and the C3 Framework for Social Studies State Standards. In all instances, students must provide precise textual evidence when answering questions about the text.

Common Core Curriculum

To understand what Common Core close reading looks like in practice, we may turn to the EngageNY Common Core Curriculum. With approximately $26 million of its Race to the Top grant, the New York State Department of Education (NYSED) directed the writing of an open-access curriculum that school districts across the country have adopted and adapted. As of June 2016, there have been more than 45 million downloads of EngageNY lessons, modules, units, sources, and texts.[14] Given that Coleman's organization Student Achievement Partners collaborated with NYSED on the modules, the curriculum provides perhaps the most closely Common Core–aligned lesson plans available.

If one goes to the Common Core Curriculum home page (www .engageny.org/common-core-curriculum), one sees a column with an ELA curriculum for each grade. Clicking on Grade 5, one arrives at a curriculum map for the full year. Module 1 is titled "Stories of Human Rights," and its focus is on "becoming a close reader and writing to learn."

The 654-page module tells teachers and students what to do and say for nearly all of the time period covered. Grade 5: Module 1: Unit 1: Lesson 1, "Getting Ready to Learn about Human Rights," tells teachers to spend the first ten minutes engaging students to think about the words "human" and "rights"; check in for the next five minutes employing the Fist to Five strategy; use the next five minutes to scan the Universal Declaration of Human Rights (UDHR); and spend fifteen minutes doing a close reading of Article 1 of the UDHR. The teacher says: "The process we just went through is called close reading. There are lots of different ways to read closely, but the main point is to figure out specific words and read more than once to get a deeper understanding of a hard text." Then, the class spends ten minutes on the close reading anchor chart; returns to thinking about "human rights" for ten minutes; and then debriefs for five minutes before the teacher gives out homework.

The modules include many assignments that require students to provide evidence from the text. For example, the tenth lesson in this module is "Analyzing a Firsthand Human Rights Account for Connections to Specific Articles of the UDHR." The teacher distributes strips of paper that include firsthand accounts of human rights and strips of paper that include UDHR articles. The teacher then says: "Your challenge is to sort the evidence I have given you. As a group, spread out the UDHR article strips. Then, read each evidence strip and discuss what article it goes with, and why." Throughout this assignment, students are expected to support their point of view with "text-based evidence." The words "text" and "evidence" appear on nearly every page of the module, and reading, discussing, and writing all revolve around finding evidence from a text.

Finally, the modules aim to prepare students for Common Core ELA tests that "ask students to analyze texts and address meaningful questions using strategic, textual details."

My argument is not that the students should not learn about the UDHR, though it is troublesome that the modules do impart a pro–United Nations viewpoint that some teachers and parents may find objectionable. Rather, my argument is that the Common Core Curriculum imposes a rigid plan and schedule on teachers and students. In theory, the Common Core standards are not a curriculum; in reality, for millions of children the Common Core Curriculum gives lockstep instructions for the entire school year. A principal once told me that his school adapts rather than adopts the modules, but that merely suggests that the Common Core Curriculum is not too prescriptive because it can be ignored. However, education reformers are developing ways—including video cameras in the classroom and high-stakes testing—that make it risky for schools or teachers to depart too far from scripts that may lead to higher student test-score growth.[15] The Common Core Curriculum places confines around what teachers and students may do in the course of the school year.

Common Core Testing

If you live in a relatively progressive school district, attend private school, or are homeschooled, do you still have to master Common Core close reading? You do if you plan to take the college entrance exams, the SAT. Furthermore, the Every Student Succeeds Act permits school districts, with state approval, to use a "nationally-recognized high school assessment" to satisfy its testing provisions.[16] The US Department of Education has already given permission to Connecticut and New Hampshire to use the SAT as their federally mandated annual test.[17] In 2015, over 1.7 million students took the SAT, and that number seems likely to rise as other states use the SAT for assessment purposes and as a requirement for admission to public institutions of higher education.[18] To paraphrase Yong Zhao: the SAT may be becoming our country's *gaokao*, the high-stakes test that determines children's college and career prospects.

Upon becoming president of the College Board, Coleman aligned the SAT with the Common Core and expedited the process to deliver it electronically. The SAT does not "over-associate with the Common Core," not least to accommodate states such as Texas and Indiana that do not officially use the standards.[19] But the SAT demands that students master close reading to score well. In this section, I show how the Evidence-Based Reading and Writing section of the SAT and the optional essay assess close reading. As a guide, I use The Princeton Review's *Cracking the New SAT: 2016 Edition*, which states, "You just need to know how to approach the text and the questions/answers in order to maximize accuracy and efficiency. It's all about the text! (No thinking!)"[20]

The Evidence-Based Reading Test requires students to answer fifty-two questions about five textual passages in sixty-five minutes. Each passage has between 500 and 750 words and ten or eleven questions. Two of the passages are about science, two are about history/social studies, and one is literature. The Educational Testing Service (ETS), the organization that makes the test for the College Board, gives the following instruction for the Reading Test: "Each passage or pair of passages is followed by a number of questions. After reading each passage or pair, choose the best answer to each question based on what is stated or implied in the passage."

Cracking the New SAT presents a few principles for students to follow as they take the reading test. One is: "**Read What You Need.** Don't read the whole passage! Use Line References and Lead Words to find the reference for the question, and then carefully read a window of about 10–12 lines (usually about 5 or 6 lines above and below the Line Reference/Lead Word) to find the answer to the question." A Line Reference is provided in the question and tells you where to look in the passage; a Lead Word requires test takers to find the evidence in the text to answer the question. In both cases, the Princeton Review's advice is that you read the questions first and then find the needed evidence in the passage. If students know what to look for, they do not need to read the entire passage to answer questions correctly.

Another principle is: **"Predict the Correct Answer.** Your prediction should come straight from the text. Don't analyze or paraphrase. Often, you'll be able to find something in the text that you can actually underline to predict the answer."[21]

Cracking the New SAT offers a sample passage, in this case about windshield damage, and types of questions the SAT will ask. They include:

- The author most likely mentions the Canadian scientist (line 22) and the Utah resident (line 26) in order to

- The author's statement that the "country moved on to building backyard fallout shelters" (lines 31–32) implies that Americans

- As used in line 41, "common" most nearly means

- According to the passage, what percent of cars in Washington suffered damage?

- Which choice provides the best evidence for the answer to the previous question?[22]

These questions mirror the ones that Coleman posed in "Cultivating Wonder," as well as the process to answer them—namely, find the lines that give the evidence to answer them. The questions also assess different anchor standards. The question about the meaning of "common," for instance, tests the fourth anchor standard: "Interpret words and phrases as they are used in a text, including determining technical, connotative, and figurative meanings, and analyze how specific word choices shape meaning or tone."

What if a question asks students to infer something? "It's still just a straight reading comprehension question. There may be a tiny bit of reading between the lines, so far as the answer will not be directly stated in the text as it will with a detail question, but there will still be plenty of evidence in the text to support the correct answer."[23]

The Common Core requires students to read like a detective. On the SAT, students demonstrate their detective skills by reading a passage, finding the evidence, and bubbling or clicking the correct answer.

The Writing and Language Test consists of forty-four multiple choice questions that students have thirty-five minutes to complete. The passages have certain words underlined and students choose a replacement, if any, that is better grammatically and stylistically. "Can you really test writing on a multiple-choice test?" the Princeton Review asks. "We'd say no, but ETS and the College Board seem to think the answer is yes. . . . If you like to read and/or write, the SAT may frustrate you a bit because it may seem to boil writing down to a couple of dull rules."[24]

Coleman once videotaped a lesson plan on the Gettysburg Address that requires students to answer questions about the document relying solely on the text, not historical context or personal responses to it. One Student Achievement Partners representative explains why teachers should teach in this way: "Whatever you've heard about assessments coming down the pike, you're not going to be able to introduce the text to the kids."[25] That is sage advice for the SAT: students have to read a passage and follow the rules of close reading, not share their thoughts or feelings.

The final ELA section of the SAT is an optional essay. Students have fifty minutes to read a text and write an analysis of an author's argument. The ETS Essay Rubric says that the highest scoring answer "makes skillful use of textual evidence" and "contains relevant, sufficient, and strategically chosen support for claim(s) or point(s) made."[26] The best way to score well on the SAT essay is to master the rules of close reading, including, above all, citing the text to build an argument.[27]

The previous two passages have shown what students do—in the classroom, for homework, and preparing for college entrance exams—in the Common Core era. For more examples, look at Pearson, McGraw-Hill, or Core Knowledge curricula or take the ACT or

New York State Regents exams. In virtually all Common Core ELA materials, students read a short textual passage and then answer questions about it, correct it, or write an essay about it. In the next section, we ask: What kinds of political skills and dispositions does close reading teach? And should democrats support the nationalization of this kind of education?

A Progressive Critique of Close Reading

People have been reading texts closely for millennia, citing passages from the text to justify an interpretation. That is not what is distinctive about Common Core close reading. The Common Core requires "text-dependent" and "text-specific" answers. Put another way: the Common Core demands that students quote the text and not add or change anything in their re-presentation. In this section, I reconstruct John Dewey's warning about how this pedagogy does not prepare children for active citizenship.

In *Democracy and Education* Dewey discusses a type of pedagogue he calls The Schoolmaster. The Schoolmaster believes "the business of the educator is, first, to select the proper material . . . and, secondly, to arrange the sequence of subsequent presentations on the basis of the store of ideas secured by prior transactions."[28] The Schoolmaster creates a curriculum map that does not change or respond to the particular children in the classroom. From a Deweyan perspective, E. D. Hirsch Jr. is a Schoolmaster for designing the Core Knowledge curriculum that teaches children cultural literacy in a fixed progression. But Coleman is also a Schoolmaster for identifying standards that all children—regardless of their language skills, learning abilities, or particular interests—must be able to master by a fixed point in time. Close reading does not give children an opportunity to disagree with the textual passage: they must simply answer questions or write analyses.

Dewey explains the pedagogical problem of this approach: "It exaggerates beyond reason the possibilities of consciously formulated and used methods, and underestimates the role of vital, unconscious attitudes. It insists upon the old, the past, and passes lightly over the operation of the genuinely novel and unforeseeable."[29] Members of the New York Regents Standards Review and Revision Initiative made this point in a letter to David Coleman about the Common Core in February 2010: "While its broad statements often express a rounded view of educational goals and vision, its specifics again and again reduce the objectives to what can be measured, to simplistic conceptions of literacy, and to a narrowly instrumental view of language. . . . The document . . . seems constricted to items that can be measured by conventional standardized instruments. . . . School seems like a very grim place—Gradgrind lives."[30]

Why does this matter politically? Dewey thinks that democracy as a way of life, rather than merely a means to select leaders, cannot survive if a few private school students are taught to think and lead while public school students are taught to follow orders. "Democracy cannot flourish where the chief influences in selecting subject matter of instruction are utilitarian ends narrowly conceived for the masses, and for the higher education of the few, the traditions of a specialized cultivated class. The notion that the 'essentials' of elementary education are the three R's mechanically treated, is based upon ignorance of the essentials needed for realization of democratic ideals."[31] We have already seen that Common Core curricula and testing require students to repeat verbatim passages from a text. Quoting accurately is not thinking; thinking is a more complicated and fluid process that requires experimenting to solve a problem.[32] From a Deweyan perspective, it is troubling that many political and economic elites who advocate the Common Core choose a different pedagogical model for their own children.[33]

This book does not present a comprehensive alternative to national education standards, in part because a democratic conception of education counsels against it. For Dewey, the educational experience takes place among singular teachers and students in a particular community at a precise moment in time. Dewey does provide general principles to structure democratic education. "From the side of the child, it is a question of seeing how his experience already contains within itself elements . . . of just the same sort as those entering into the formulated study." "From the side of the studies, it is a question of interpreting them as outgrowths of forces operating in the child's life."[34] Think of a graph where the x-axis is a child's age and the y-axis is wisdom. The point is to bring a child to the highest point over time, to have each year bring a child to a new plateau of knowledge. What drives the student to ascend as high as possible is interest, a desire to scratch an intellectual itch or solve a practical problem. Progressive educators seek to awaken something inside children that drives them to learn as much about the world as possible. The goal is for children to master and put their own mark on a body of knowledge. "Let the child's nature fulfil [sic] its own destiny revealed to you in whatever of science and art and industry the world now holds as its own."[35]

Dewey's term of art for education standards in *Democracy and Education* is "aims." "An aim implies an orderly and ordered activity, one in which the order consists in the progressive completing of a process."[36] Dewey recommends that schools make short-, medium-, and long-term aims, on two conditions. The people affected have to have a decisive voice in creating the aims, and the aims must remain flexible. "A good aim surveys the present state of experience of pupils, and forming a tentative plan of treatment, keeps the plan constantly in view and yet modifies it as conditions develop. The aim, in short, is experimental, and hence constantly growing as it is tested in action."[37] For Dewey, people in the school and community should have an ongoing conversation about teaching and learning literacy. In the year of a presidential election, for example, students can make a journal about the race; in the year of the Olympics, they can write a history of the games. And so forth.

For Dewey, it is important that personalized education be available to children of every race, gender, ethnicity, and class. Democracy means that each person gets to develop their talents and interests to the fullest so that everyone in the community can benefit. Think of a potluck where each person makes his or her signature dish, and everybody gets to taste and enjoy the other dishes. Conversely, "lack of the free and equitable intercourse which springs from a variety of shared interests makes intellectual stimulation unbalanced."[38] Democratic education creates joy because we all get to delight in each other's accomplishments; a stratified education system creates class antagonism and mutual contempt. Dewey and other progressive educators hoped that public education could be a place to model a democratic society, one not governed by the laws of the market.

From a Deweyan perspective, Common Core close reading teaches children to place their own interests and concerns in a separate compartment of their mind than the one completing the assignment. According to Daniel Katz, chair of the Department of Educational Studies at Seton Hall University, "If children in classrooms using the CCSS English standards learn to love reading on a deeply personal and affective level and develop a life long [sic] relationship with reading as a means of self exploration, it will be in spite of those standards, not because of them."[39]

In *Teaching to Exceed the English Language Arts Common Core Standards*, three professors of English Education—Richard Beach, Amanda Haertling Thein, and Allen Webb—claim that progressive educators can still work with the Common Core ELA standards. The book acknowledges that political and economic elites have led the Common Core State Standards to impose a market, or neoliberal, vision of education reform on the country. "The CCSS reading and writing standards can readily lend themselves to adopting a formalist approach that emphasizes teaching the structures of narrative, argumentative, informational, and explanatory texts."[40] The authors wish that the standards had a more critical and multicultural edge, one that helps classroom teachers use the pedagogical principles of John Dewey or Paulo Freire. The authors themselves favor a "critical inquiry" approach that "invites students into the curriculum making process."[41] But given that the Common Core appears to be here to stay, the authors propose a compromise solution: teachers can maintain autonomy by exceeding the standards.[42]

The authors quote the Introduction to the Common Core State Standards: "A great deal is left to the discretion of teachers and curriculum developers. The aim of the Standards is to articulate the fundamentals, not to set out an exhaustive list or a set of restrictions that limits what can be taught beyond what is specified therein."[43] The authors want to help classroom teachers navigate the current education environment, finding or creating opportunities for critical inquiry, critical literacy, and multicultural explorations.

It is good to make the best of a bad situation. Still, progressive public schooling may not survive the Common Core era; Dewey and Coleman are far apart on the conservative-progressive pedagogical spectrum. Dewey envisioned a Copernican revolution in education whereby the entire educational apparatus would revolve around each unique student.[44] At the 2011 Albany event, Coleman said, "People really don't give a shit about what you feel or what you think. What they instead care about is can you make an argument with evidence, is there something verifiable behind what you're saying or what you think or feel that you can demonstrate to me."[45] In our present historical moment, Common Core advocates have two kinds of weapons to use against their progressive adversaries. One is to regulate inputs such as teacher certification, professional development, curricula, or classroom evaluations. Another is to hold schools and teachers accountable for outputs—namely, test-score growth. We no longer live in an era when teachers are free to close the classroom door and do what they like. Unless educators, parents, and policymakers come to its defense, America's partial experiment with Deweyan educational principles in public education will end.[46]

Conclusion

In my school district, I would love to advocate a Deweyan model of English education in which teachers, librarians, parents, and students participate in a running dialogue about what books kids should be reading and what assignments would best spark a desire to read or write. I wish that the district had not decided to adopt/adapt the EngageNY modules in the 2016–2017 academic year. Rather than use their training or initiative to craft lesson plans, teachers print the modules and mostly follow the instructions. When I talk to veteran teachers, I grieve at the things lost in the Common Core era, including events like Thanksgiving feasts or Friday projects—the things that are often what children remember most about their elementary education.

In our historical moment, education progressives should not look to the federal government for redress. Political scientists have shown that we live in an era of economic-elite domination where the affluent have much more influence than the majority in shaping federal policy. The rich often get their way in policy debates when they disagree with the majority, but the opposite almost never happens.[47] And the rich today, as a rule, favor the standards, testing, and accountability paradigm. That was true during the Obama administration, and it will likely hold true during the Trump administration and for the foreseeable future. In the conclusion, I explain how the Every Student Succeeds Act makes it difficult for states to choose academic content standards that differ substantially from the Common Core.

It is hard to imagine education progressives writing national education standards in the next few decades. Rather than pursue this agenda, I recommend that education progressives defend and work within America's tradition of local education control. Democratic education, according to Deborah Meier, requires that young people "grow up in the midst of adults who are making hard decisions and exercising mature judgment in the face of disagreements."[48]—in other words, in an environment where ordinary people hold real power over matters such as curriculum. This holds true as much in urban school districts with mostly black and Latino students as it does in wealthier and whiter suburbs.[49] Some might say that we need to trust experts to handle something as important as education standards, but this chapter has argued that America has made a mistake by putting nearly all of its education eggs in the Common Core basket. Put bluntly: our country has nationalized a pedagogy that requires students to regurgitate from the text to earn a good score on standardized tests. This skill does not prepare children for selective liberal arts colleges, thinking careers, or democratic citizenship.

In the conclusion, I elaborate my vision of returning meaningful education control to communities. Now, we consider the other major topic covered in the Common Core standards: mathematics.

FOUR

Math Standards, Understanding, and College and Career Readiness

··

This chapter, on the Common Core State Standards for Mathematics, begins by discussing the history of the standards and how they balance procedural mastery and conceptual understanding. I then show how the standards teach and assess mathematical understanding by looking at the EngageNY Common Core Curriculum and the SAT. The chapter considers two critiques of the Common Core math standards. The emphasis on showing your work may challenge mathematically gifted students who lack language skills, and the placement of Algebra I in ninth grade makes it difficult for students to enter a pathway to take calculus in high school or major in a STEM field in college. In conclusion, I argue that democracies should not try to end the math wars and instead should encourage a healthy competition between philosophies of math education.

The History of the Common Core Math Standards
··

In an article for the *New England Journal of Public Policy*, Jason Zimba, a founding partner of Student Achievement Partners and a lead writer of the Common Core math standards, explains the development and design of the standards.[1]

In the early 2000s, Achieve led the American Diploma Project to identify a progression of literacy and numeracy standards that students need to learn to be college and career ready. Near the end of the decade, the Council of Chief State School Officers (CCSSO) and the National Governors Association (NGA) joined the effort to create a new set of national education standards. In April 2009, Achieve, the CCSSO, and the NGA assembled a committee that produced a document called "College and Career Readiness Standards," and in September 2009, these groups assembled committees to develop the Common Core State Standards. The three-member writing team included Zimba, Phil Daro, and William McCallum. Fifty-one people participated on the Mathematics Work Team, twenty-two people on the Mathematics Feedback Group, and twenty-nine people on the Validation Committee.

The Common Core standards-writing process built upon the American Diploma Project, high-performing countries' standards documents, national reports, peer-reviewed articles, and research on mathematics education. The process also involved communication between the writing team and state departments of education and representatives from teachers unions and the National Council for the Teaching of Mathematics (NCTM). On March 10, 2010, the public draft of the standards was released; groups and individuals commented; and on June 2, 2010, the Common Core Standards were released. In 2010 and 2011, most American states and territories adopted the standards.

The Common Core standards envision mathematical excellence as a combination of three things. First, students must demonstrate procedural mastery. "You are not excellent in math unless you can get the right answer without hesitation. The standards require students to know the addition and multiplication facts from memory. No standards in the Common Core require students to invent algorithms."[2] The Common Core requires students to become fluent with the standard algorithm for all four operations: addition, subtraction, multiplication, and division.

Second, students must have conceptual understanding. "Concepts matter because students who cannot think mathematically will typically sooner or later forget how to solve problems they once knew how to solve. So it is important for the sake of math achievement to address concepts in adequate depth." The Common Core emphasizes arithmetic in the early grades to prepare children to study algebra.[3]

Finally, students must master the ability to apply math to solve problems.

For over a century, there has been a math war between conservatives-traditionalists and progressives-reformers, those who emphasize memorization versus those who demand that students understand what they are doing. Zimba sides with the conservatives on the question of memory: "Generally, conservative education thinkers celebrate memory, while progressives denigrate it. I side with the conservatives. Too often, progressives seem to want something for nothing: all the glories of critical thinking but without strong investment in the machinery it runs on. Progressives also appear terrified of making the students sweat through varieties of learning they might not like."[4]

Zimba seems to side with progressives on the need for students to understand what they are doing: "Teachers are right that students will perform better if they think about mathematics. And, in addition, we have to hold on tightly to the part of math education that serves at the command of memory. Rather than a replacement for answer-getting or skill, concepts are a strategy for raising achievement."[5]

At this point, Zimba turns to a set of other important topics, including the process of aligning textbooks with the Common Core. For our purposes, we will read the standards document itself for insight into how the Common Core balances procedural mastery and conceptual understanding and defines college and career readiness.

The Philosophy of Common Core Math

The Introduction to the Common Core State Standards for Mathematics says the standards "define what students should understand

and be able to do in their study of mathematics. Asking a student to understand something means asking a teacher to assess whether the student has understood it. But what does mathematical understanding look like? One hallmark of mathematical understanding is the ability to justify, in a way appropriate to the student's mathematical maturity, why a particular mathematical statement is true or where a mathematical rule comes from."

The Introduction continues: "There is a world of difference between a student who can summon a mnemonic device to expand a product such as $(a+b)(x+y)$ and a student who can explain where the mnemonic comes from. The student who can explain the rule understands the mathematics and may have a better chance to succeed at a less familiar task such as expanding $(a+b+c)(x+y)$. Mathematical understanding and procedural skill are equally important, and both are assessable using mathematical tasks of sufficient richness."[6]

The document then explains the Standards for Mathematical Practice (SMP). Some standards lean more toward progressive math ideology. One SMP says that students should be able to "construct viable arguments and critique the reasoning of others." This standard presses students to ask "why?" and "how do you know?" even about apparently simple things such as "How do you *know* that $8+4=12$? Or consider this version: If you couldn't remember what $8+4$ was for a moment, how could you figure it out?" Another SMP states that students need to "make sense of problems and persevere in solving them." The reason for this standard is that "students need to make sense of problems when they do math. The meaning of a *problem* varies widely from kindergarten through high school, but making sense of problems is important throughout. 'Does this make sense?' is an important question for students to ask themselves."[7]

Other SMP standards lean toward the conservative side of the spectrum. One SMP, for instance, requires students to attend to precision. "Mathematically proficient students try to communicate precisely to others. They try to use clear definitions in discussion with others and in their own reasoning. They state the meaning of the symbols they choose, including using the equal sign consistently and appropriately. They are careful about specifying units of measure, and labeling axes to clarify the correspondence with quantities in a problem. They calculate accurately and efficiently, express numerical answers with a degree of precision appropriate for the problem context." Students need to get precise answers to mathematical questions, and they also need to use precise definitions. "A circle is a round shape" is not a precise definition; "a circle is the set of points in a plane that are the same distance from a common point, called the center" is. Occasionally, students may want to use back-of-the-envelope calculations, and the standards that make up the SMP encourage students to ask, "Is it good enough?"[8]

The SMP standards are general statements about what students should do to think and work like mathematicians, but they do not say much that can be directly imparted or assessed. The SMP informs the content standards, which detail what students should learn when.

The Standards for Mathematical Content compose the bulk of the document and sequentially structure student expectations in domains such as counting and cardinality, operations and algebraic thinking, number and operation in base ten, measurement and data, and geometry. According to the document, standards with the word *understand* signal a connection between practices and content. Students are not supposed to just enter and compute data; they need to understand what they are doing and why. "Students who lack understanding of a topic may rely on procedures too heavily. Without a flexible base from which to work, they may be less likely to consider analogous problems, represent problems coherently, justify conclusions, apply the mathematics to practical situations, use technology mindfully to work with the mathematics, explain the mathematics accurately to other students, step back for an overview, or deviate from a known procedure to find a shortcut." The goal is not just to have students master calculations that they will perform only on standardized tests; the goal is to have them think in ways that will prepare them for college, careers, and life.

In grades K–8, the standards are the same for all students. The document notes that the standards may pose challenges to English language learners and students with special needs, but says that the solution is school-level support such as screen reader technology. "All students must have the opportunity to learn and meet the same high standards if they are to access the knowledge and skills necessary in their post-school lives." The document does not directly discuss how to teach mathematically gifted children, in part because Common Core proponents think the standards are already close to gifted education pedagogy.[9]

The standards document changes at the end of middle school. In grades K–8, the standards are organized by grade level. According to Appendix A of the standards document, the high school standards are organized by conceptual categories "showing the body of knowledge students should learn in each category to be college and career ready, and to be prepared to study more advanced mathematics." Options one and two cover algebra, geometry, probability, and statistics; the difference is whether the courses are organized traditionally by subject or integrated into general mathematics courses. Options three (traditional) and four (integrated) enable students to reach calculus by their senior year if the pathway is "compacted," that is, if "students would complete the content of 7th grade, 8th grade, and the High School Algebra I course in grades 7 (Compacted 7th Grade) and 8 (8th Grade Algebra I)."[10]

There is a limit to how much standards documents reveal about their impact on the classroom or on flesh-and-blood children. To bring us closer to seeing what the Common Core means in practice, we turn to curricula and assessments designed by lead writers of the Common Core.

Common Core Curriculum

The New York State Education Department used approximately $26 million of its Race to the Top grant to partner with Student

Achievement Partners to create a Common Core Curriculum, also known as Eureka Math.[11] According to the Eureka Math homepage, it is the most widely used math curriculum in the United States, it is the only curriculum to align fully with the Common Core, and the Common Core textbook alignment tool EQuIP designates many of its lessons as exemplars.[12] In this section, we examine how the curriculum introduces students to fractions in order to see how the Common Core balances procedural understanding and conceptual mastery.[13]

If one goes to the EngageNY website (www.engageny.org /mathematics), one can find modules, or lesson plans, that cover the entirety of pre-K to eighth grade, after which the curriculum separates into pathways. The modules are "marked by in-depth focus on fewer topics" and integrate the Common Core Learning Standards, "rigorous classroom reasoning, extended classroom time devoted to practice and reflection through extensive problem sets, and high expectations for mastery." In pre-K through fifth grade, students progress through a comprehensive math education program called "A Story of Units."

According to the Common Core domain progression, fractions are a focus of grades 3–5 and lay the foundation for the number system covered in grades 6–8. Grade 3, Module 5, is on "Fractions as Numbers on the Number Line." In this thirty-five-day module, students learn to understand that fractions are equal partitions of a whole.

Topic A is "partitioning a whole into equal parts," And Lesson 1's objective is to "specify and partition a whole into equal parts, identifying and counting unit fractions using concrete models." The module suggests that this lesson should dedicate twelve minutes to fluency practice, eight minutes to an application problem, thirty-two minutes to concept development, and eight minutes for students to debrief.

For the first twelve minutes of class, students group-count by four and practice multiplying by four and eight.

For the next eight minutes, students measure the length of a book and other items using inches or centimeters and noticing the difference between the two units.

For the subsequent thirty-two minutes, students work on concept development. Initially, students partition fraction strips into equal parts, then they do a similar exercise, partitioning a whole amount of liquid into equal parts. The instructions tell the teacher (T) and students (S) what to say throughout the lesson, including how to mark, measure, connect, fold, and think about the fraction strips.

In the next ten minutes, students do a Problem Set. This particular assignment invokes Standard for Mathematical Practice 5: "Use appropriate tools strategically." Teachers may assign these questions as homework. As can be seen from the assignment, the third-graders have to draw pictures, write their answers as complete sentences, and explain what they notice and how they came up with an answer (figure 4.1).

For five of the final eight minutes, the teacher invites students to reflect on and process the lesson. In the final three minutes, students complete an Exit Ticket to help the teacher assess student understanding of the concepts and plan future lessons.

We have covered a small percentage of the material covered in the EngageNY math curriculum that provides this kind of detailed instruction for virtually every math class from pre-K to the end of middle school. But we have an example of how the Common Core requires students to arrive at precise answers and use and explain the concepts that guide their math reasoning.

Common Core Testing

The College Board, according to its report, "Reach Higher: Delivering on Common Core State Standards," "has been a consistent advocate and committed collaborator in the development of Common Core State Standards. In fact, our research informed the drafting

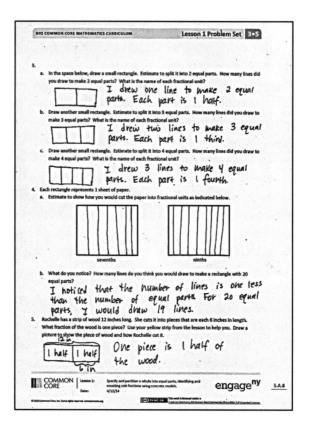

FIGURE 4.1   Excerpt from EngageNY Common Core Curriculum Grade 3 Mathematics Module 5: Fractions as Numbers on the Number Line. *Source*: EngageNY.org of the New York State Education Department

of the standards, and our experts helped guide the standards development process."[14] One of David Coleman's priorities upon becoming president of the College Board was to align the SAT with the Common Core standards.[15] Given that the Every Student Succeeds Act permits states to use the SAT for its federally required tests, as well as the test's role in admission for many institutions of higher education, the SAT is an important Common Core test for many students around the country. How does the SAT assess procedural mastery and conceptual understanding? We may use the Princeton Review *Cracking the New SAT, 2016 Edition* as a guide.

The SAT math test is eighty minutes long. Students have twenty-five minutes to work on the no-calculator Section and fifty-five minutes to work on the calculator section. The math test covers (1) Heart of Algebra, (2) Problem Solving and Data Analysis, (3) Passport to Advanced Math, and (4) Additional Topics in Math. Educational Testing Service, the organization that writes the SAT questions following instructions from the College Board, says that the math test covers "all mathematical practices." The Princeton Review responds, "Fortunately for you, there is no way one test can cover all mathematical concepts. The SAT Math Test is actually a brief test of arithmetic, algebra, and a bit of geometry—when we say a 'bit,' we mean it. There are only 6 geometry questions at most on the test."[16]

The SAT math section is composed of multiple-choice questions and Grid-Ins. A Grid-In requires students to provide answers by bubbling in numbers or symbols in a column. The SAT gives credit only for a correct answer, not for showing one's work. How, then, does the SAT measure conceptual understanding?

One way, according to an article in *The Atlantic*, is by "replacing logic-based word problems with questions that more directly probe students' knowledge of mathematical concepts." The article quotes the founder of a test prep company: "The current SAT asks questions where the material is remarkably simple, but students have to figure out what exactly they are asking for. . . . Let's say it's a question about how much a driver should budget for gas, but they will add in all this other information. The car has a trailer attached, and the driver will be driving 15 percent faster than usual, and gas prices have gone up. The math is really easy it's just figuring out what they are asking that is really tough."[17]

The Princeton Review makes a similar point: "There are questions that are so wordy and deceptive that reading carefully is a much more important skill than properly using a calculator."[18] Many of the SAT questions are word problems, and the Princeton Review's advice is: "**Cut the Fat**. ETS will frequently add unnecessary information to word problems. . . . If you find the unnecessary information distracting, you can lightly strike through it."[19]

For example, in 2016 the College Board released a practice question that requires students to help a laundry service "buying detergent and fabric softener from its supplier." The paragraph has five sentences with information about the weight of shipments, how much containers of fabric softener and detergent cost, and so forth, before asking students, "Which of the following systems of inequalities best represents this situation?"[20] On the one hand, students must display the Common Core ELA skill of close reading to decode this passage; on the other, they must discern which information is relevant or irrelevant to arriving at a correct answer. Like the SAT Evidence-Based Reading and Writing Section, the SAT Math Test provides opportunities for students to apply math to real-life applications in finance, business, social science, and natural science.[21]

In the next two sections, I consider critiques of the Common Core math standards. My argument is not that the Common Core covers useless material, or that every Common Core–aligned activity, assignment, or test is a waste of time. My point is that thoughtful, informed people see flaws with the Common Core standards themselves, and a democracy should create space for them to influence the curriculum in some communities. On Madisonian grounds, I also contend that one faction should not hold a de facto monopoly on college entrance exams. Thus, I am sympathetic to attempts to create alternatives to the Common Core–aligned SAT or ACT.

Here, then, are two critiques of the Common Core math standards that, in my view, are sufficiently weighty to contest their nationalization.

The Problem with Explaining Your Math

To understand how the Common Core standards expectation of conceptual mastery may place roadblocks in the pathways of mathematically talented students, we may turn to a 2015 article in *The Atlantic* called, "Explaining Your Math: Unnecessary at Best, Encumbering at Worst,"[22] by Katharine Beals, a lecturer at the University of Pennsylvania Graduate School of Education, and Barry Garelick, a middle and high school math teacher in California.

Beals and Garelick note that the Common Core asks student to justify, in a way appropriate to their maturity, why a mathematical statement is true or where a mathematical rule comes from. They then cite several examples, similar to the EngageNY modules cited above, that require students to write a narrative summary of how they solved the problem.

Beals and Garelick argue that writing explanations sometimes turns routine problems into "unnecessary and tedious" assignments. They observe that many students first solve the problems in their heads and then write a narrative using "verbalisms" they have been taught. It is not that the students now understand how their mathematical minds work; it is that they can sufficiently repeat the words that the teacher has told them they need to do if they want a good grade.

Beals and Garelick argue that students need to learn to do math before they can meaningfully explain what they are doing. Once a word problem has been translated into a mathematical representation, "the entirety of its mathematically relevant content is condensed onto abstract symbols, freeing working memory and unleashing the power of pure mathematics. That is, information and procedures that have . . . become automatic frees up working memory. With working memory less burdened, the student can focus on solving the problem at hand. Thus, requiring explanations beyond the mathematics itself distracts and diverts students away from the convenience and power of abstraction. Mandatory demonstrations of 'mathematical understanding,' in other words, can impede the 'doing' of actual mathematics." Many students need to do math for a while before the lightbulb flashes and they can explain how they arrived at the answers.

English language learners who are otherwise good at math now face setbacks because they cannot write grammatically correct sentences explaining their math reasoning.

Likewise, many mathematically gifted children on the autism spectrum can fail math courses or tests because they cannot verbalize their thought process. Beals and Garelick remark that many great mathematicians have exhibited characteristics of Asperger syndrome; now the inability to explain one's methods "has morphed into an unprecedented liability."

For Beals and Garelick, there is no reason to make all children jump through hoops or penalize English learners or children on the autism spectrum. "If a student can consistently solve a variety of problems, that student likely has some level of mathematical understanding. . . . It's far from clear whether a general requirement to accompany all solutions with verbal explanations provides a more accurate measurement of mathematical understanding than the answers themselves and any work the student has produced along the way."

Does the Common Core necessitate constructivist pedagogy? In a blog responding to Garelick's critique, Jason Zimba says no.[23] The Common Core standards mention only the standard algorithm and no other algorithms, and educators are free to introduce the standard algorithm earlier than fourth grade. True, the Common Core challenges "pedagogies that neglect the key math concepts that are essential foundations for algebra and higher mathematics." But Zimba thinks that "good, traditional pedagogy" is compatible with the Common Core standards.

In the comments to the blog, conservative math educators Wayne Bishop and Ze'ev Wurman argue that the Common Core math standards are in the progressive camp. Bishop says, "The preamble chapter Standards for Mathematical Practice belie[s] the entire content standards themselves. Instead of routine practicing for some level of retention and automaticity (including 'cook-book' word problems) it is an endorsement for the math ed industry's beloved constructivism. Pure pedagogy and probably by design." Wurman says, "I find it hard to believe that Zimba truly expects kids to master addition and subtraction to fluency in one fell swoop in grade 4, yet that [is] what the standards he authored seemingly expect. After all, Common Core has no problem repeating exhortations about its 'drawings' and 'strategies' year after year . . . it's just the standard algorithms that are supposed to spring fully-formed into student brains in grade 4 without any prior mention."

Garelick, Bishop, and Wurman contend that the Common Core standards express a certain vision of mathematics that is at odds with a more traditionalist vision. The EngageNY Common Core Curriculum instructs students to write sentences to demonstrate metacognition, and the SAT may thwart students who excel at math but do not understand "wordy and deceptive" word questions. The Common Core requires students to explain their math, and this may be a problem for some students. In the conclusion, I explain more why I think that the Common Core should not crowd out other ways to teach mathematics.

What Kind of College or Career?

A second critique of the Common Core math standards is made by two members of the Common Core Validation Committee who refused to sign off on the document: R. James Milgram, professor emeritus of mathematics at Stanford University, and Sandra Stotsky, professor emerita in the Department of Education Reform at the University of Arkansas. In their 2013 white paper, "Can this Country Survive Common Core's College Readiness Level?" Milgram and Stotsky argue that the Common Core prepares most students for community college or vocational programs, not science, technology, engineering, or mathematics (STEM) careers.

According to Milgram and Stotsky, the early-grade Common Core standards progress too slowly. By the end of fifth grade, students' knowledge of arithmetic and algebra will be more than a year behind the early-grade expectations of high-achieving countries. By the end of seventh grade, students will be two years behind their international peers. Many high-performing countries cover some of Algebra I and Geometry in grades 6, 7, and 8, and by the end of ninth grade, students will have finished all of Algebra I, most of Algebra II, and Geometry, including proofs, at a high level of sophistication. The Common Core makes no provision for Algebra I by eighth grade.[24]

The high school standards also set a low bar. The standards end with Algebra II, and there is little coverage of trigonometry. A public comment draft of the Common Core standards included place-markers (or "stubs") that indicated additional topics that would be included in the standards to prepare students to study calculus in high school. These stubs included limits and continuity, differential calculus, applications of derivatives, integral calculus, applications of integration, and infinite series. Milgram and Stotsky note, however, that "except for a small amount of the trigonometry material, not one of the seven stubs . . . or any precalculus material remains in Common Core's final mathematics standards, even as a stub."[25]

That is the heart of the matter for Milgram and Stotsky: Common Core math does not prepare children for STEM careers. According to government data, "it is extremely rare for students who begin their undergraduate years with coursework in precalculus or an even lower level of mathematical knowledge to achieve a bachelor's degree in a STEM area."[26]

Is it fair to say that the Common Core sets low mathematics expectations for most students? Addressing this question, Milgram and Stotsky cite a 2013 report from the National Center on Education and the Economy, "What Does It Really Mean to Be College and Work Ready?" Phil Daro, a member of the Common Core math writing team, co-chaired the mathematics panel, and the report was funded by the Bill & Melinda Gates Foundation as part of their College Ready Education strategy. According to the report, "it is clear that for a substantial majority of high school graduates, being ready to be successful in the first year of a typical community college program is tantamount to being ready for both college and work." The report argues that students simply need elementary and middle school mathematics to major in accounting, automotive technology, business, or criminal justice at a community college. Most students do not need Algebra II, a prerequisite for precalculus and calculus courses but that only a small fraction of people use for their careers.[27]

Many parents, Stotsky and Milgram assert, believe that Common Core math is preparing their children for professions such as engineer and doctor, not automotive technology or criminal justice. "At this time we can conclude only that a gigantic fraud has been perpetrated on this country, in particular on parents, by those developing, promoting, or endorsing Common Core's standards."[28]

Common Core defenders, including Jason Zimba, bristle at traditionalist criticisms. The American Mathematical Association, the Mathematical Association of America, and the National Association of Mathematicians endorse the Common Core. Scholars have compared the Common Core standards favorably to high-performing countries in grades K–8. Critics "want to call students college ready only if they go beyond Algebra II to take trigonometry, precalculus, or calculus. . . . [What critics] think of as 'college ready' is what I might call 'STEM ready.' I think it makes sense to most people that college readiness and STEM readiness are two different things. The mathematical demands that students face in college will vary dramatically depending on whether they are pursuing a STEM major or not."[29] Students can still take calculus in high school under the Common Core.

In Westchester County, New York, according to an article in a local newspaper, the Common Core will lower the number of students who take calculus in high school. Local education authorities no longer permit many seventh or eighth graders to take algebra. The reason, according to Marla Gardner, director of curriculum and instructional services for the regional Board of Cooperative Educational Services (BOCES), is that "we want kids to get a firm foundation in Common Core math, particularly in eighth grade, so they can be successful later." Slowing down the math progression early means that it must be accelerated later, which is why BOCES is developing a 3-in-2 program—a two-year high school program for grades 10 and 11 that combines three one-year courses in geometry, algebra 2/trigonometry, and precalculus.[30]

New York High School Principal of the Year Carol Burris explains the consequences of 3-in-2 programs: "The study of calculus in high school will be reserved only for the elite. By eliminating algebra in grade 8, moving it to grade 9 and then compacting the study of geometry, advanced algebra, trigonometry and pre-calculus into two courses, teachers will be required to teach at breakneck speed. Few students will be able to keep up. Those who do will only get surface exposure to the topics. Our math teachers already complain that there is not enough time to adequately teach all of the topics in algebra 2/trigonometry. To add pre-calculus to the mix, as well as topics excluded by the Common Core, would make the course inaccessible to all but a handful of students."[31] The facts on the ground confirm the Milgram-Stotsky critique of the Common Core.

Conclusion

Should math class involve teachers demonstrating, and students practicing, formal symbolic procedures? Or should math class be focused on teachers providing students with opportunities to solve problems, discuss mathematics, and construct math ideas? In the math wars, conservatives-traditionalists tend to favor the former answer, and reformers-progressives the latter.[32] One purpose of the Common Core is to end the math wars. In a public talk, Bill Gates said, "Should Georgia have a different railroad width than anybody else? Should they teach multiplication in a different way? Oh, that's brilliant. Who came up with that idea?" He continued, "Common Core is, to me, a very basic idea that kids should be taught what they're going to be tested on and that we should have great curriculum material."[33] According to Ze'ev Wurman, a US Department of Education official under George W. Bush, "As long as Common Core is around, there won't be conventional curriculum 'wars' anymore—there will be nuclear holocausts, lasting winner-take-all kind of events. Whoever captures Common Core and its assessments leaves nothing behind."[34] Wurman exaggerates only slightly: most students today study Common Core math to prepare for Common Core–aligned high-stakes tests.[35]

There may be advantages to national education standards in mathematics, including creating a national market for education innovations and for teachers to share their expertise across state lines. Students, including those in military families, may also move from one school district to another without missing a beat.[36] But there are disadvantages as well.

In this chapter, we have considered thoughtful, informed critiques of the Common Core math standards themselves. The standards' conception of understanding creates a barrier for many students who are mathematically gifted but lack linguistic skills, including English language learners and children on the autism spectrum. The standards do not reach algebra in time for many high school students to study precalculus or calculus and thus major in a STEM discipline in college. The Common Core standards emphasize basic and applied math skills that may be necessary for community college but are insufficient for students who want to become engineers or doctors. A compressed high school math pathway enables few students to study advanced mathematics in time to earn admission to a prestigious institution of higher education. If critics are even partially correct in their concerns about the Common Core, we are making a mistake by placing nearly all of our mathematical education eggs in one basket.

As a political theorist, my main concern is what happens to the political fiber of a country that adopts national education standards. Today, math educators who disagree with the Common Core cannot influence public school math instruction in a meaningful way in many parts of the country. Nakonia Hayes, a retired public school teacher and principal, for instance, wrote an article for *The Federalist* praising John Saxon's original, pre–Common Core Advanced Mathematics textbooks. Hayes describes Saxon's philosophy of math education as "old-fashioned memorization and repetition"; she quotes students in Arizona, Utah, and Georgia who speak about him with reverence and say that he changed their views about math. Hayes says schools that use Saxon math score highly on standardized tests and notes that the movie "Stand and Deliver" was about a math instructor who taught Hispanic students Saxon math. She concludes: "Reformists have become so embedded with political and philanthropic support because of Common Core that it is unlikely any one person can fight their ideology as vehemently and as publicized as Saxon did."[37] Hayes is just one of the many traditionalist math educators who know, and grieve, that they have little voice in the Common Core era.

There is also the parental outcry against the standards. Karen Lamoreaux's critique of early–Common Core math, made before the Arkansas State Board of Education in December 2013, has been watched over three million times on YouTube. One Maryland father was arrested for yelling at a public education forum that the Common Core would not prepare his children to go to Harvard.[38] The comedians Stephen Colbert and Louis C. K. have criticized the Common Core standards, and many people complain on social media about their children's Common Core homework.

Zimba and others say that these homework assignments predate the Common Core or are not necessarily aligned.[39] But as we have seen, the EngageNY Common Core Curriculum has the kinds of assignments that people complain about on social media. And some mathematicians and math educators think that parents are right that the Common Core does not prepare children for STEM careers.

Political science research has shown that states that have gone the furthest in standards-based education reform witness parents participating less in schools and the community.[40] By nationalizing the Common Core math standards, everyone who disagrees has little recourse other than to move, and even that step probably will not work.[41] As a result, many math educators and parents feel alienated from the political process. They believe, correctly, that a small group of philanthropists and political insiders coordinated a plan to impose their vision of mathematical education on the entire coun-

try.[42] And if political scientists are right about the political consequences of education reform, then these educational conservatives
are likely to exit the political process or vote for politicians who
promise to get rid of the Common Core.

The quality of the Common Core standards does not outweigh
the political consequences of driving away many people from the
democratic process. A large, diverse democracy should encourage a
healthy competition among philosophies of math education.

FIVE

Science Standards, Scientific Unity, and the Problem of Sustainability

··

This chapter discusses the Next Generation Science Standards (NGSS). It begins by explaining the origin, main features, and vision of the NGSS. Next, I describe how *A Framework for K–12 Science Education*—the National Research Council report that provides the scientific foundation for the NGSS—addresses the question of implementation. I anticipate what the NGSS online assessments will look like by studying the science questions on the Programme for International Student Assessment (PISA). The chapter considers two critiques of the NGSS: that it marginalizes material that cannot be tested easily on computers, and that the account of sustainability places too much trust in engineering fixes. I argue the standards can lead to expensive reforms that can displace, as in New York, more hands-on conceptions of science education. The conclusion contends that there are pedagogical and civic advantages to an educational culture that sustains diverse models of scientific education.

The History of the Next Generation Science Standards

··

There are three main steps by which the NGSS has come into being as America's de facto national science education standards.[1]

The National Research Council partnered with the American Association for the Advancement of Science, the National Science

Teachers Association, and Achieve to develop *A Framework for K–12 Science Education* (hereafter *Framework*). The *Framework* articulates expectations for what students should be able to know and do in science by the end of certain grade bands and by the time they graduate from high school. It identifies multiple reasons for the importance and timeliness of the *Framework* and the subsequent standards. All students should appreciate "the beauty and wonder" of science. Students should be able to make informed decisions about public policies on scientific matters. They should be "careful consumers of scientific and technological information related to their everyday lives." Students should acquire the ability and desire to learn about science after graduation. And all young people need the skills to enter, if they wish, careers in science, technology, engineering, and math (STEM).[2] In July 2011, the National Research Council released the *Framework* that provides the foundation for the NGSS.

Achieve, one of the groups that led the Common Core State Standards Initiative, managed 26 states and 40 writers in the process of writing the NGSS. Stephen Pruitt, then senior vice president for Achieve and presently the Kentucky Commissioner of Education, coordinated the development of the NGSS.[3] Achieve also partnered with the US Education Delivery Institute to write an NGSS Adoption and Implementation Workbook to provide guidance and templates for leadership teams to help states adopt and implement the standards.[4] The final version of the NGSS was released in April 2013.

States had opportunities to revise and contribute to the NGSS before adopting it. Achieve, for instance, selected New York in September 2011 to be an NGSS Lead State Partner. In that role, New York made a commitment to "give serious consideration to adopting the resulting *Next Generation Science Standards* as presented," to "participate in Multi-State Action Committee meetings . . . to discuss issues regarding adoption and implementation of the new standards, to "publicly announce the state is part of the effort to draft new science standards and make transparent the state's process for outreach/receiving feedback during the process," and to provide

K. Forces and Interactions: Pushes and Pulls

Students who demonstrate understanding can:

K-PS2-1. **Plan and conduct an investigation to compare the effects of different strengths or different directions of pushes and pulls on the motion of an object.** [Clarification Statement: Examples of pushes or pulls could include a string attached to an object being pulled, a person pushing an object, a person stopping a rolling ball, and two objects colliding and pushing on each other.] [Assessment Boundary: Assessment is limited to different relative strengths or different directions, but not both at the same time. Assessment does not include non-contact pushes or pulls such as those produced by magnets.]

K-PS2-2. **Analyze data to determine if a design solution works as intended to change the speed or direction of an object with a push or a pull.*** [Clarification Statement: Examples of problems requiring a solution could include having a marble or other object move a certain distance, follow a particular path, and knock down other objects. Examples of solutions could include tools such as a ramp to increase the speed of the object and a structure that would cause an object such as a marble or ball to turn.] [Assessment Boundary: Assessment does not include friction as a mechanism for change in speed.]

The performance expectations above were developed using the following elements from the NRC document *A Framework for K–12 Science Education:*

Science and Engineering Practices	Disciplinary Core Ideas	Crosscutting Concepts
Planning and Carrying Out Investigations Planning and carrying out investigations to answer questions or test solutions to problems in K–2 builds on prior experiences and progresses to simple investigations, based on fair tests, which provide data to support explanations or design solutions. • With guidance, plan and conduct an investigation in collaboration with peers. (K-PS2-1) **Analyzing and Interpreting Data** Analyzing data in K–2 builds on prior experiences and progresses to collecting, recording, and sharing observations. • Analyze data from tests of an object or tool to determine if it works as intended. (K-PS2-2) ⎯⎯⎯⎯⎯⎯⎯⎯⎯⎯⎯⎯⎯⎯⎯ *Connections to Nature of Science* **Scientific Investigations Use a Variety of Methods** • Scientists use different ways to study the world. (K-PS2-1)	**PS2.A: Forces and Motion** • Pushes and pulls can have different strengths and directions. (K-PS2-1),(K-PS2-2) • Pushing or pulling on an object can change the speed or direction of its motion and can start or stop it. (K-PS2-1),(K-PS2-2) **PS2.B: Types of Interactions** • When objects touch or collide, they push on one another and can change motion. (K-PS2-1) **PS3.C: Relationship Between Energy and Forces** • (NYSED) A push or a pull may cause stationary objects to move, and a stronger push or pull in the same or opposite direction makes an object in motion speed up or slow down more quickly. *(secondary to K-PS2-1)* **ETS1.A: Defining Engineering Problems** • A situation that people want to change or create can be approached as a problem to be solved through engineering. Such problems may have many acceptable solutions. *(secondary to K-PS2-2)*	**Cause and Effect** • Simple tests can be designed to gather evidence to support or refute student ideas about causes. (K-PS2-1),(K-PS2-2)

Connections to other DCIs in kindergarten: **K.ETS1.A** (K-PS2-2); **K.ETS1.B** (K-PS2-2)

Articulation of DCIs across grade-levels: **2.ETS1.B** (K-PS2-2); **3.PS2.A** (K-PS2-1),(K-PS2-2); **3.PS2.B** (K-PS2-1); **4.PS3.A** (K-PS2-1); **4.ETS1.A** (K-PS2-2)

Common Core State Standards Connections:

ELA/Literacy –
RI.K.1 With prompting and support, ask and answer questions about key details in a text. *(K-PS2-2)*
W.K.7 Participate in shared research and writing projects (e.g., explore a number of books by a favorite author and express opinions about them). (K-PS2-1)
SL.K.3 Ask and answer questions in order to seek help, get information, or clarify something that is not understood. *(K-PS2-2)*

Mathematics –
MP.2 Reason abstractly and quantitatively. *(K-PS2-1)*
K.MD.A.1 Describe measurable attributes of objects, such as length or weight. Describe several measurable attributes of a single object. *(K-PS2-1)*
K.MD.A.2 Directly compare two objects with a measurable attribute in common, to see which object has "more of"/"less of" the attribute, and describe the difference. (K-PS2-1)

a timeline for when it will adopt science standards.[5] In January 2015, the New York Board of Regents approved a Statewide Strategic Plan for Science, and in the summer of 2015, New York state science educators prepared a preliminary draft of state science learning standards based on the 2013 survey, the *Framework*, and the Next Generation Science Standards. In December 2016, the Board of Regents adopted the New York State P–12 Science Learning Standards—which are nearly identical to the NGSS, including the color, layout, and terminology (figure 5.1).

What is the relationship between the NGSS and the Common Core? The NGSS Executive Summary explains that many of the same people worked on both sets of standards: "Science is a quantitative discipline, which means it is important for educators to ensure that students' learning in science coheres well with their learning in mathematics. To achieve this alignment, the NGSS development team has worked with Common Core State Standards in Mathematics (CCSSM) writing team members to help ensure that the NGSS do not outpace or otherwise misalign to the grade-by-grade standards in CCSSM. Every effort has been made to ensure consistency." In addition: "Literacy skills are critical to building knowledge in science. To ensure the CCSS literacy standards work in tandem with the specific content demands outlined in the NGSS, the NGSS development team worked with the CCSS writing team to identify key literacy connections to the specific content demands outlined in the NGSS."[6] Thus, the NGSS provides Common Core State Standards Connections on the bottom of each page. "The NGSS are aligned with the CCSS to ensure a symbiotic pace of learning in all content areas."[7]

The Philosophy of the NGSS

The NGSS identifies performance expectations of what students should be able to know and do by the end of instruction. The standards are grade-specific in elementary school and break up into grade bands for middle school. The four domains of the NGSS are Physical Science (PS), Life Science (LS), Earth and Space Science (ESS), and Engineering, Technology, and Applications of Science (ETS). The standards proceed in order of grade or grade band, domain, disciplinary core idea, and performance expectation. For example, K–PS2–I is a performance expectation for kindergartners in the physical sciences covering the disciplinary core idea of forces and interactions. Thus, kindergartners at the end of the unit should be able to "plan and conduct an investigation to compare the effects of different strengths or different directions of pushes and pulls on the motion of an object." The performance expectations include clarifications and assessment boundaries.[8]

In figure 5.1, the middle boxes of the NGSS identify the three dimensions of science education outlined in the *Framework*. These are the distinguishing feature of the NGSS and express its vision of a high-quality science education.

The disciplinary core ideas (the box in the middle) identify the scientific content that students should learn. The *Framework* dedicates over a hundred pages to explaining the core and component ideas in each of the four domains. In the physical sciences, for instance, the *Framework* says that students should learn the core idea of matter and its interactions as well as the component ideas about the structure and properties of matter, chemical reactions, and nuclear processes. Or, for the life sciences, students should learn the following about molecules and organisms: their structure and function, the growth and development of organisms, the organization for matter and energy flow in organisms, and information processing. The goal of the *Framework* is not to identify all of the facts that students should know but to provide them with "sufficient core knowledge so that they can later acquire additional information on their own."[9]

The crosscutting concepts (the box on the right) "have application across all domains of science."[10] Crosscutting concepts include patterns, cause and effect, systems and system models, energy and matter, structure and function, and stability and change.

Science and engineering practices (the box on the left) describe "(a) the major practices that scientists employ as they investigate and build models and theories about the world and (b) a key set of engineering practices that engineers use as they design and build systems."[11] Learning practices enable students, from an early age, to do science and become scientists. The practices include asking questions, defining problems, using models, planning investigations, interpreting data, using mathematics, constructing explanations and designing solutions, engaging in argument from evidence, and obtaining information.

In chapter 3, I noted that Common Core close reading, and its focus on providing precise evidence from the text, reappears in the NGSS. For instance, practices 7 and 8 restate, in a disciplinary context, the need for students to provide evidence from a text:

Engaging in Argument from Evidence
In science, reasoning and argument are essential for identifying the strengths and weaknesses of a line of reasoning and for finding the best explanation for a natural phenomenon. Scientists must defend their explanations, formulate evidence based on a solid foundation of data, [and] examine their own understanding in light of the evidence.

Obtaining, Evaluating, and Communicating Information
Science requires the ability to derive meaning from scientific texts (such as papers, the Internet, symposia, and lectures), to evaluate the scientific validity of the information thus acquired, and to integrate that information.[12]

The *Framework* links the practices to the Common Core standards. "Because writing is one of the primary means of communicating in the scientific community, learning how to produce scientific texts is as essential to developing an understanding of science as learning how to draw is to appreciating the skill of the visual artist."[13] The Common Core ELA and math standards intertwine with the NGSS, above all with the expectation that students engage in argument using evidence from the text.[14]

Implementing the NGSS

How the NGSS will transform science education in the United States is the topic of chapter 10 of the *Framework*: "Standards provide a vision for teaching and learning, but the vision cannot be realized unless the standards permeate the education system and guide curriculum, instruction, teacher preparation and professional development, and student assessment."[15] "Successful implementation requires that all of the components across the levels cohere or work together in a harmonious or logical way to support the new vision. This kind of system-wide coherence is difficult to achieve, yet it is essential to the success of standards-based science education."[16] The chapter offers ideas on how to arrange each major component of the education system around the NGSS.

Curricula, naturally, should integrate the NGSS practices, concepts, ideas, and progressions.

Learning and instruction should also be informed by the NGSS. In general, the *Framework* posits that progressive conceptions of "inquiry" are too ambiguous to use as a guide for building a science education system.[17] "The expectation is that students generate and interpret evidence and develop explanations of the natural world through sustained investigations. However, such investigations must be carefully selected to link to important scientific ideas, and they must also be structured with attention to the kinds of support that students will need."[18]

The initial preparation and professional development of teachers should train them in best practices for delivering the NGSS.

Finally, the NGSS should guide assessment: "Designing high-quality science assessments that are consistent with the framework, that satisfy the different purposes of assessment, and that function in the varying contexts of use is an important goal, which will require attention and investment to achieve."[19] The *Framework* holds that paper and pencil multiple-choice exams are too crude to measure performance expectations, and "hands on tasks can be cumbersome and expensive. Computer-based assessment offers a promising alternative. Simulations are being designed to measure not only deep conceptual understanding but also the science practices that are difficult to assess using paper-and-pencil tests or hands-on laboratory tasks." Particularly promising are online science assessments used by the Programme for International Student Assessment (PISA).[20]

The PISA Precedent

The Every Student Succeeds Act maintains No Child Left Behind's requirement that states, to receive Title I funds, must administer science tests at least once in elementary, middle, and high school. According to a May 2017 *Education Week* article, states are presently designing NGSS online assessments, and the "test-delivery platforms will look similar to those being used for math and reading tests aligned with the Common Core State Standards."[21] Given that what gets tested gets taught, NGSS assessment will influence what happens in the science classroom. The Next Generation Science Assessment task portal provides a few in-development online assessment tasks.[22] To get a sense of what NGSS assessments will look like, I recommend that we study the PISA 2015 released field trial cognitive items.[23]

The PISA science assessment tests competencies, actions that "convey the idea that the scientifically literate person both understands and is capable of undertaking a basic set of practices which are essential for scientific literacy."[24] These competencies include being able to explain phenomena scientifically, evaluate and design scientific inquiry, and interpret data and evidence scientifically. Much like the NGSS practices, PISA requires students to "distinguish between arguments which are based on scientific evidence and theory and those based on other considerations" and "evaluate scientific arguments and evidence from different sources (e.g., newspaper, Internet, journals)."[25]

The PISA tests types of scientific knowledge in a number of contexts. The types of knowledge include content (physical systems, living systems, and earth and space science), procedures (methods and practices), and epistemic knowledge (how beliefs in science are justified). The contexts include health, natural resources, the environment, hazards, and the frontiers of science and technology. For both NGSS and PISA, the "emphasis is on what students can do instead of on what they have memorized."[26]

Here are a few observations about PISA. The science assessment uses colorful graphics, and taking the test feels like playing a video game. The right answer to almost all of the questions is in the accompanying passages; in other words, PISA tests close reading of scientific informational texts. Students do not need to memorize the names of flowers, minerals, animals, processes, geographic locations, or formulas to do well on the tests.[27] If students have mastered the competencies—preeminently decoding text—then they should be able to select the right multiple-choice answer (for the low cognitive demand questions) or write in the requested information (for the medium and high cognitive demand questions). Finally, one can prepare for the PISA. When I first tried to answer questions, I often was uncertain about my choices. But upon reading the explanations, I learned the correct way to fill in a PISA question that involves tables of data, maps, or textual passages. With test preparation, students can score highly on PISA with minimal scientific content knowledge or practical experience with, say, building a structure, combining chemicals in a beaker, or dissecting a frog.

For example, here is a released item from the 2015 test on volcanic eruptions. The tested competency is "Interpret Data and Evidence Scientifically" and the cognitive demand is low. The context is "Global-Hazards" and the question tests procedural knowledge (figure 5.2).

Students do not need to know about volcanoes, the Ring of Fire, or geography before taking the test to answer it correctly. Further-

Unit CS644 *Volcanic Eruptions*
Unit Overview

This released unit focuses on the distribution pattern of volcanoes and the impact of volcanic eruptions on climate and the atmosphere. Stimulus materials include a map showing the location of volcanoes and earthquakes around the globe and graphs illustrating the impact that volcanic eruptions have on the amount of solar radiation that reaches Earth's surface and on carbon dioxide concentrations in the atmosphere.

Unit 644 *Volcanic Eruptions*
Released Item #1

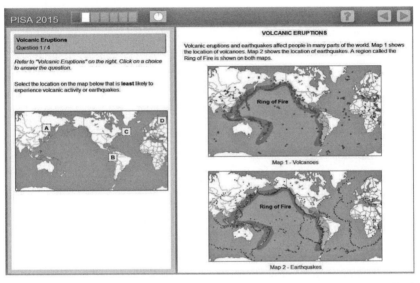

Students must interpret data presented on a map to identify the location least likely to experience volcanic activity or earthquakes. The correct response is map location *D*, over northern Europe.

FIGURE 5.2   *PISA 2015 Released Field Trial Cognitive Items on Volcanic Eruptions.*
Source: OECD PISA

more, this question could be tweaked and presented for many other scientific topics too. For instance, the question could be about bees and clover fields, and the student would simply have to select the letter that is farthest from the ring of pesticide in the center of the image.

This pattern persists for questions with a medium cognitive demand. For instance, there is a unit on "Bee Colony Collapse Disorder" that has two paragraphs of informational text about the relationship between bees, birds, and the food they eat. The question for Unit CS600 asks: "Why might the disappearance of bees result in a decline in the bird population?" The question tests the competency "Explain Phenomena Scientifically" in the context of "Local/National-Environmental Quality." "To correctly answer this question, students must provide an explanation that states or implies that a flower cannot produce seeds without pollination." The word "pollination" does not appear in the text, so it might be advantageous for students to have that knowledge in advance. And yet, there is enough information in the text so a student could answer that when bees "feed on the nectar of the sunflower" they help create the seeds that birds eat. This implies that a flower cannot produce seeds without pollination. A savvy test taker could find key words from the text and incorporate them into the answer. Students do not need to know specifics about birds, bee colonies, or pollination to get a correct answer.

The pattern persists for questions with a high cognitive demand. Unit 623, "Running in Hot Weather," asks students to perform a simulation based on information about air temperature, air humidity, drinking water, sweat volume, water loss, and body temperature. There is a picture of a man running in the sunshine and images of a beaker collecting sweat, a graph of water loss percentage, and a thermometer to measure body temperature. The question asks, "Do you expect that it would be safe or unsafe to run while drinking water with the air humidity at 50% and air temperature of 40°C?" The question requires students to add data to a chart, run the simulation, learn that a runner would suffer from heat stroke at both 40 percent and 60 percent humidity at 40°C and therefore infer that a runner may suffer heat stroke at 50 percent humidity and 40°C. The question tests the competency "Evaluate and Design Scientific Enquiry" in the context of "Personal-Health and Disease." This question is more of a logic problem, or a brainteaser, than a measure of scientific content knowledge.

Shortly after the publication of the final version of the NGSS, the Thomas B. Fordham Institute published a critique of the standards, arguing that the focus on practices relegates content knowledge to secondary status and that the standards place too much emphasis on writing.[28] Here I suggest why that is the case: the *Framework* makes clear that the NGSS coordinators had the PISA online assessments in mind even before writing the standards. The Common Core standards, the NGSS practices, and the PISA competencies all emphasize skills that can be tested by means of online standardized tests, above all providing evidence from a text. In the next section, we consider an argument why the NGSS's focus on testable practices leads to a poor science education.

A Procrustean Account of Science

In Greek mythology Procrustes was a bandit who would cut off his victims' limbs so that they would fit on his cart. In *Challenging Science Standards: A Skeptical Critique of the Quest for Unity*, Charles R. Ault Jr. argues that the NGSS is procrustean insofar as it cuts off elements of science that do not fit within standards-based education reform.[29]

Ault is professor emeritus at Lewis & Clark Graduate School of Education and has taught courses in science education, field geology, natural history, and curriculum theory. In his book, Ault criticizes the NGSS's notion of practices and crosscutting concepts that somehow recur throughout all of the sciences. The NGSS is the most recent version of the question to identify "the" scientific method that children should learn in schools. "Generation after generation, national reforms in science teaching have overemphasized abstract, unifying concepts descended with modification from scientific method. Believing that standardization is prerequisite to educational accountability, reformers promote one-size-fits-all thinking that tends to stereotype science as experimental method."[30]

Ault identifies four main constituencies that coalesce on standardizing science education. State bureaucrats advocate common standards because it makes possible measuring educational outcomes and holding teachers and students accountable. Disciplinary scientists, particularly in lower-prestige disciplines, appreciate a universal account of scientific method that places all scientists on the same plane. Corporate entities push education reforms that create new markets. And science educators feel compelled, in order to prepare all students for social responsibility and possibly STEM careers, to repeat an old story about the unity of the sciences.

The NGSS, Ault's account, pays lip service to differences between scientific disciplines but then demands that all science educators conform to the NGSS template. "The NGSS's generic lists oversimplify what scientists do and disturbingly promote ignorance of how diverse methods and distinctive concepts combine to achieve different ends." Unless curriculum designers satisfy the conditions of the NGSS alignment rubric, "lesson plans and curricula proposals will receive low scores, whatever innovative ties to actual science it might embody. The evaluation process shoehorns all sciences into a one-size-fits-all framework."[31]

Ault's thesis is that the sciences are different and that it is a myth that one package of concepts and practices can cover all of them. "Studying landslides is very different from doing x-ray diffraction: climate science is unlike medical research. Methods of inquiry in each context correspond to the demands of the problem, and the events of interest vary in fundamental ways; each landslide is unique; all x-rays are the same. . . . The methods for studying diverse phenomena must match their distinctive challenges."[32] Much of *Challenging Science Standards* elaborates on how the sciences differ and confound any attempt to shoehorn them into one checklist of qualities. For instance, geologists, paleontologists, evolutionary biologists, and cosmologists employ the historical style of science that addresses "complex, singular objects unfolding through time: one earth, one universe, one history of life." The problems and methods of the historical sciences differ from those of the experimental sciences that dominate most accounts of the scientific method.[33]

The solution for Ault is for science educators to honor the differences between the scientific disciplines. "The progression of core ideas ought to culminate in mastery of a small number of conceptions that organize thinking in well-defined contexts, keeping concepts linked to methods of inquiry in each step."[34] Ault presents this solution as a revision of the NGSS rather than its destruction: "Respecting diversity can rescue the NGSS's overly ambitious portrait of scientific unity through careful development of core disciplinary ideas and their assessment in terms of disciplined—not universal—approaches to thinking and doing science."[35] One can anticipate, however, why Achieve would decline Ault's proposal to create unique curricula for each of the scientific branches: it would defeat the purpose of systemic education reform. The *Framework* makes clear that the purpose of the NGSS is to create large-scale standardized testing, not a boutique introduction to the different scientific disciplines.

According to Ault, however, the NGSS presently does not honor the specificity of actual scientific work. By prioritizing what can be taught and graded in a uniform manner, it does not prepare children to study or work in certain important areas of science.[36]

The Problem of Sustainability

According to the *Framework*, NGSS standards will help students address "major challenges that confront society today, such as generating sufficient energy, preventing and treating diseases, maintaining supplies of clean water and food, and solving the problems of global environmental change."[37]

Some individuals and organizations protest the NGSS because its standards "impose alarmist global warming ideas on children from kindergarten forward, and assume people are a net negative for the Earth while ignoring the truth that humans have both positive and negative effects on the environment."[38] In response, some defenders of the NGSS say this critique provides evidence for why we need to accelerate adoption of the standards.[39]

This section considers the argument that the NGSS may be objectionable for the opposite reason, namely, that it fails to prepare students to think and act in ways that are adequate to the sustainability challenge. According to University of Wisconsin–Madison professors Noah Weeth Feinstein and Kathryn L. Kirchgasler, the NGSS advances "an oversimplified idea of sustainability that diminishes its social and ethical dimensions" and leads "students to systematically misinterpret and underestimate the challenges that confront their local, regional, and global communities."[40]

To make this case, Feinstein and Kirchgasler examine the theme of sustainability throughout the NGSS and contextualize the standards in broader debates about sustainability among scientists, philosophers, social scientists, and public policy scholars. According to their analysis, the NGSS expresses universalism, scientism, and technocentrism.

Universalism is the idea that science concerns a global system and an undifferentiated mass of humanity. The standards mention spheres such as the atmosphere, the hydrosphere, the geosphere, and so forth, but there is little mention of political history, specific locations, or political units. According to Feinstein and Kirchgasler, the problem with universalism is that it "obscures the fact that sustainability-related problems afflict some humans more than others and that human actions, embodied in contemporary policies and social institutions, contribute to poverty, hunger, and environmental vulnerability."[41] In other words, by bracketing questions of politics, the NGSS suggests that all human beings are equally responsible for climate change and will equally feel its effects. The authors, and many people around the world, contest those claims.

Scientism maintains that scientists should lead the response to problems such as predicting natural hazards, managing natural resources, or reducing human impact on the environment. "In these examples, the NGSS explicitly emphasizes the value of quantitative scientific methods for understanding sustainability and responding to real-world problems." Feinstein and Kirchgasler point out, however, that problems such as flooding are as much economic, political, social, and cultural as they are scientific.[42]

Technocentrism is the faith that science, technology, and engineering can solve the problems of sustainability. A disciplinary core idea states that scientists and engineers can develop technologies that produce less pollution. That idea is plausible, but it can lead to more controversial ideas such as requiring students to consider "large-scale geoengineering design solutions" like pumping carbon dioxide into the ocean. "Taken as a whole, this vision of sustainability resembles *ecological modernization*, a technology-centered, managerial perspective on sustainability."[43]

The problem with ecological modernization is that it leads students to look for quick technological fixes to problems that may require long-term attention; it also marginalizes the "ethical and political dimensions of emerging sustainability challenges." Furthermore, ecological modernization can foster an antidemocratic approach to addressing environmental problems. Scientism does not prepare students "for the political realities of a pluralist, democratic society that must balance the needs of multiple groups and integrate science with other sources of knowledge."[44] For instance, many people ought to have a say in policies regarding bioengineering, not just scientists, who may ignore the perspectives of small farmers or indigenous communities that resist the project of genetically modifying food.[45]

If Feinstein and Kirchgasler are right, then nationalizing the NGSS would mean that young people will not have the right tools to address global climate change. They will grasp for technological solutions and resist making hard trade-offs or sacrifices. Oil and gas companies such as Chevron and ExxonMobil support the standards,[46] and one organizing team member of the NGSS explains that "fossil-fuel exploration and development will need to push more into more challenging work environments to maintain and expand supply."[47] There may be a danger in nationalizing a scientific vision that wants to intensify humanity's extraction of fossil fuel. We need to make sure that at least a sizable body of students can learn other ways of thinking and acting in the world.

One of the main arguments for national science standards is that they promise to raise the bar for all children, but particularly for groups that have been unfairly neglected in the past: girls, children of color, and poor children. In this section, I argue that the NGSS can lead to expensive reforms that crowd out other valuable ways to study science. The *Framework* emphasizes the importance of on-screen learning and assessment, but equity arguments could just as easily stress the need for teacher-crafted, hands-on science learning activities.

The NGSS has steep financial and opportunity costs. Properly implementing the NGSS will require new curricula, assessments, technology to administer the assessments, accountability systems, teacher certification, and professional development. And the *Framework* commends the use of "modern computer-based visualization tools."[48]

In "The Child and the Curriculum," John Dewey makes a prescient critique of science education that does not give children opportunities to manipulate physical objects with their hands or see nature unmediated by technology. According to Dewey, children need to experience the world to understand it. Conversely, "the lack of any organic connection with what the child has already seen and felt and loved makes the material purely formal and symbolic."[49] Consider, for example, the PISA 2015 computer-based question about sustainable fish farming.[50] The question asks students to click and drag icons (common sole, ragworms, shellfish, and marsh grass) to different tanks on an experimental fish farm to harvest fish in a sustainable way. When I took the test, I found the exercise fun and informative, but I am an adult who has spent much of his life at the seaside and on boats. I have touched, breathed, smelled, heard, and seen with my own eyes the elements of this question. For a test taker who has not, the material is purely formal and symbolic. This question may mean nothing to many children, and the information learned from the question may be quickly forgotten by many kids who do not care about the subject. As a parent, I would rather my young children go on a field trip to an aquarium, the beach, or a lake than learn about fish on a computer.

In New York, the Next Generation Science Standards will replace science standards and materials that had a more Deweyan bent. Consider, for example, SCIENCE21, "an inquiry-based elementary school science program, developed 'by teachers for teachers,' that includes comprehensive curriculum guides, materials kits, and staff development services." According to the manual for administrators, SCIENCE21 is "an inquiry-based program" in which "students study the natural world and construct meaning and explanations based upon evidence that they derive from their activities." SCIENCE21 has a Material Center that assembles over twelve thousand science kits a year, and each kit includes materials such as balances, microscopes, magnets, thermometers, powders, liquids, wire, bulbs, cups, soil, seed, batteries, and wires. "Field trips to nature centers, museums, science centers, zoos, and the like can greatly enrich children's experiences in SCIENCE21," and "parents, guardians, or other community members who have particular expertise in the areas under study can be invited into the classroom to enrich and enhance student learning." In both its language and its concrete activities, SCIENCE21 evinces a commitment to Dewey's pedagogical principle that human beings learn with all of their senses and not just their eyes.[51]

There is a chance that New York will keep using the kits, at least for a little while. But it bears repeating that the *Framework* says that "administering and scoring these hands-on tasks can be cumbersome and expensive" and that "computer-based assessments offer a promising alternative."[52] The National Research Council designed the NGSS with computer-based simulations and assessments in mind—not kits, not field trips, not guest lecturers. There is reason to believe that the NGSS will make the quality of science education worse in New York, particularly for students whose families cannot supplement the curriculum with experiential activities.[53]

Conclusion

According to the Fordham Institute, the NGSS standards are better than the science standards in twenty-six states but worse than those in twenty states. The report acknowledges the benefits of common science standards—including comparability, portability, and economies of scale—but responds, "'Common' standards are not inherently superior to the work of individual states—and 'improved' standards can come from multiple directions."[54] I agree with this critique. National education standards can create an educational monoculture that has bad pedagogical and civic consequences.

My point in this chapter is not to advocate a particular vision of science education. Rather, I advocate the democratic principle of local control. Ordinary citizens do not have to become experts in all aspects of pedagogy to exercise meaningful power in the schools. Instead, ordinary people can choose among the options created by experts.[55] In this chapter, I have cited experts who have identified flaws with the NGSS and indicated what a better science education looks like. These experts should have a chance to persuade citizens to choose their vision.

As a parent, I would prefer to have my children do hands-on science activities, meet scientists, compete in science fairs, visit university labs, and the like, rather than prepare for or take online assessments. In a democracy, parents, educators, and community members should have the power to make that decision.

SIX

History Standards, American Identity, and the Politics of Storytelling

....

This chapter discusses the country's de facto honors US history standards: the Advanced Placement U.S. History (APUSH) curriculum framework. Initially, the chapter reviews the history of APUSH and the 2014 and 2015 revisions of the framework. My explanation of the 2015 framework concentrates on its account of historical thinking skills that require students to perform a close reading of historical documents. The chapter then considers a conservative critique of the framework that emphasizes gender, class, racial, and ethnic identities rather than a shared American identity. To understand how APUSH impacts honors US history courses, I study the framework and the Princeton Review's *Cracking the AP U.S. History Exam* and show how the framework requires students to master Common Core close reading and prescribed thematic learning objectives and historical concepts. The framework is geared toward preparing students for the APUSH standardized exam and gives teachers and students few opportunities to challenge its political ideology, particularly as the College Board has the power to audit curricula. In the conclusion, I argue that democracies should empower local communities to debate and decide together how to interpret and impart history.

In an article called "Privilege, Equity, and the Advanced Placement Program: Tug of War," Jack Schneider provides a history of the Advanced Placement Program that provides the background to current controversies surrounding APUSH.[1]

In the 1950s, John Kemper, the headmaster of Phillips Andover, coordinated the School and College Study of Admission with Advanced Standing with two other elite private schools, Exeter and Lawrenceville, as well as Harvard, Princeton, and Yale. The goal was to create an academic program for the strongest students to study advanced material at high-status public or private schools. In 1955, Charles Keller became the first director of the Advanced Placement Program to be administered by the College Board, the organization that also runs the SAT. The goal was to provide a "teacher-proof curriculum" that enabled even poorly trained teachers to impart university-level knowledge to bright students.[2] Initially, the AP program primarily served rich white children destined for elite institutions of higher education.

In the 1960s, the AP program became more concerned with equity. Some reformers thought the AP program could be a way for socially disadvantaged children to get the same type of education as children were able to get at prestigious suburban or private high schools. In the 1980s, states such as West Virginia and Arkansas began to invest in AP programs, and in the 1998–1999 school year, the US federal government spent $2.7 million to subsidize teacher training and student participation in the AP program.[3] More recently, in 2013 the US Department of Education awarded states more than $28 million to cover fees for low-income students to take AP tests.[4]

According to Schneider, "one unintended but foreseeable consequence of the expansion of AP has been a declining level of prestige and achievement associated with the program."[5] In the early days of the AP program, a few hundred privileged students took the exam for the intrinsic rewards of the challenge; today, millions of students take the exam for the purpose, among others, of getting college credits to reduce college costs. Elite private schools such as the Concord Academy are crafting their own history courses to distinguish themselves from the many schools that use the AP program. Ironically, the College Board's push for greater equity may lead to inequitable outcomes as the AP turns into "just another packaged curriculum."[6]

In the spring of 2012, Common Core architect David Coleman became president of the College Board. In an interview at the time, Coleman said, "We have a crisis in education, and over the next few years, the main thing on the College Board's agenda is to deliver its social mission. . . . The College Board is not just about measuring and testing, but designing high-quality curriculum."[7] In a 2011 report, the College Board said that it "has been a strong advocate for and played an active role in the development of the Common Core State Standards." The College Board helped draft the standards and provided guidance on the Common Core Advisory Committee. The Common Core "strongly reflects the guiding mission and values of the College Board, as well as our programs and services."[8] The College Board has continued to align the Advanced Placement program with the Common Core.[9]

In 2014, the College Board released a new APUSH curriculum framework. The Republican National Committee said the framework "emphasizes negative aspects of our nation's history while omitting or minimizing positive aspects." Other conservative scholars and pundits argued that the framework imparted an anti-American, leftist worldview. In 2015, responding to these criticisms, the College Board released a revised APUSH curriculum framework, explaining, "We heard from and engaged with a wide range of stakeholders over the past year as part of our public review process. Teachers and historians, parents and students, and other concerned citizens and public officials from across the country all provided feedback."[10] We will return to the debate about the political ideology embedded in APUSH, but first we look at the framework itself.

Historical Thinking Skills

The APUSH course covers American history from approximately 1491 to the present. Much like the tripartite division of the Next Generation Science Standards, the APUSH curriculum framework covers thinking skills, themes, and content (table 6.1).[11]

In earlier chapters, I argued that the Common Core ELA anchor standards and the NGSS practices are the keys to understanding the respective standards. Here, I argue that the historical thinking skills are the distinguishing feature of the new APUSH curriculum framework. Like the anchor standards and the practices, the historical thinking skills emphasize close reading of informational texts.

The framework presents the historical thinking skills in two ways: from the perspective of a history practitioner and for the purpose of identifying proficiency expectations that can be measured on the AP test.

One historical thinking skill category is analyzing historical sources and evidence: "Historical thinking involves the ability to describe, select, and evaluate relevant evidence about the past from di-

TABLE 6.1 *APUSH Curriculum Framework*

Thinking skills	Themes	Content
Analyzing primary and secondary sources	American and national identity	Significant events, individuals, developments, and processes in nine historical periods
Making historical comparisons	Migration and settlement	
Chronological reasoning	Politics and power	
Argumentation	Work, exchange, and technology	
	America in the world	
	Geography and the environment	
	Culture and society	

Source: College Board, *AP Course and Exam Description*

verse sources . . . and draw conclusions about their relevance to different historical issues." The parallel historical thinking skill proficiency expectation requires students to "explain the relevance of the author's point of view, author's purpose, audience, format or medium, and/or historical context as well as the interaction among these features, to demonstrate understanding of the significance of a primary source."[12]

Another historical thinking skill category is creating and supporting a historical argument: "Historical thinking involves the ability to create an argument and support it using relevant historical evidence. . . . A persuasive historical argument requires a precise and defensible thesis or claim, supported by rigorous analysis of relevant and diverse historical evidence." The aligned proficiency expectation states that students must be able to "develop and support a historical argument, including in a written essay, through a close analysis of relevant and diverse historical evidence."[13]

These historical thinking skills resemble the Common Core State Standards for ELA & Literacy in History/Social Studies, Science, and Technical Subjects. Here, for example, are a few of the Standards for History/Social Studies in Grades 6–8:

- Cite specific textual evidence to support analysis of primary and secondary sources.

- Identify key steps in a text's description of a process related to history/social studies (e.g., how a bill becomes law, how interest rates are raised or lowered).

- Identify aspects of a text that reveal an author's point of view or purpose (e.g., loaded language, inclusion or avoidance of particular facts).

- Analyze the relationship between a primary and secondary source on the same topic.[14]

In both the Common Core standards and the AP historical thinking skills, students must cite specific textual evidence to answer questions or write essays about a text's central idea, argumentation, textual features, author's point of view, and so forth.

The emphasis on close reading is equally apparent in another set of social studies standards that have been adopted around the country: the College, Career, and Civic Life (C3) Framework for Social Studies State Standards. The National Council for the Social Studies published the C3 Framework in 2013 using "an initial guidance document" written by individuals from the Council of Chief State School Officers (CCSSO), one of the organizations that coordinated the Common Core State Standards Initiative. "The authors of the C3 Framework view the literacy skills detailed in the ELA/Literacy Common Core College and Career Readiness (CCR) Anchor Standards as establishing a foundation for inquiry in social studies, and as such all CCR Anchor Standards should be an indispensable part of any state's social studies standards."[15] In particular, the C3 Framework integrates the first Common Core ELA anchor standard's expectation of citing specific textual evidence into Dimension 3: Evaluating Sources and Using Evidence. "Through research, students hone their ability to gather and evaluate information and then use that information as evidence in a wide range of endeavors. The ELA/Literacy Common Core Standards emphasize these skills as key to an integrated model of literacy. The C3 Framework and the Indicators in Dimension 3 apply this model to social studies inquiry."[16]

In chapter 3, we saw that Common Core close reading requires children to "quote accurately" when answering questions about a text. I argued that this skill facilitates online assessments but does not prepare children to become active citizens. There is a similar dynamic at work in APUSH. Before pressing that point, we consider a conservative critique of APUSH for portraying American identity in a harsh light.

American Identity

One argument against national education standards is that they empower one group, or faction, of likeminded people to determine what and how to teach in a key subject matter. Madison's great insight in Federalist 10 and 51 is that the American political system makes it hard for any one faction to dominate in matters such as education, a power unenumerated in the Constitution and thus belonging to states or local authorities. My argument is not that the APUSH framework should express any one particular political ideology; instead, I contend that democracies ought to encourage a healthy diversity of honors US history curricula.

A public "Letter Opposing the 2014 APUSH Framework" was signed by dozens of prominent conservative academics, including James W. Caesar, a political scientist at the University of Virginia; Patrick J. Deneen, a political scientist at the University of Notre Dame; Victor Davis Hanson, a classicist at Stanford University; Ralph Ketcham, a historian at Syracuse University; and Harvey Mansfield, a political philosopher at Harvard University.

In their letter, these scholars argue that APUSH emphasizes the clash of identities in American history rather than the formation of an American identity based on the ideals of the founding generation. The 2014 framework, in its own words, focuses on "how various identities, cultures, and values have been preserved or changed in different contexts of U.S. history with special attention given to the formation of gender, class, racial and ethnic identities." According to the scholars, there is a loss when we shift from describing the American identity to a plethora of identities. "The new framework is so populated with examples of American history as the conflict between social groups, and so inattentive to the sources of national unity and cohesion, that it is hard to see how students will gain any coherent idea of what those sources might be. This does them, and us, an immense disservice."

The scholars do not advocate a simplistic account of American history that glosses over episodes of violence and racism. "We do not seek to reduce the education of our young to the inculcation of fairy tales, or of a simple, whitewashed, heroic, even hagiographical nationalist narrative. Instead, we support a course that fosters informed and reflective civic awareness, while providing a vivid sense of the grandeur and drama of its subject. . . . We believe that the study of history should expose our young students to vigorous de-bates about the nature of American exceptionalism, American iden-tity, and America's role in the world."[17]

The signatories argue that the College Board has overstepped its mandate. Previously, the College Board would provide a brief topi-cal outline instructing teachers to impart extensive factual knowl-edge of US history. "But with the new 2014 framework, the College Board has put forward a lengthy 134-page document which repudi-ates that earlier approach, centralizes control, deemphasizes content, and promotes a particular interpretation of American history."[18] It is important to understand how this point differs from the earlier one. The problem is not just that the College Board seems to pro-mote a certain ideology; it is that the detailed prescriptions of the new framework make it hard for conservative teachers to convey their understanding of US history. Surely progressives would pro-test if the shoe were on the other foot.[19]

Peter Wood, President of the National Association of Scholars, extends the conservative critique in an academic article on APUSH's conception of apprenticing and historical thinking skills: "APUSH is academic self-dramatization. It is less about teaching American history as a body of knowledge than about how fascinating it is to think about what it might mean to learn American history." Accord-ing to Wood, the historical thinking skills may cover part of what academic historians do, but APUSH's emphasis on them means that students will be not be focusing on their key task of learning Ameri-can history. "Before you get to be an 'apprentice historian,' you have to pass through the stage of novice. But APUSH, in a typical fit of postmodern narcissism, bypasses the novice stage. The student is in-vited to think of himself as smarter, more learned, and more sophis-ticated than he could possibly be."[20] The ideology and the historical thinking skills intertwine in such a way that students will learn a narrow, skewed account of American history. For instance, "the re-ligious history of the nation is treated as incidental. For that matter, the intellectual history and artistic flourishing of America get short shrift. APUSH is not exactly Marxist in outlook, but it is relentlessly materialistic."[21]

Up to now, I have suggested that APUSH is about preparing students for standardized tests and that it presents students or teachers few opportunities to challenge its implicit political ideology. To see how that it is the case, we need to study the APUSH exam.

What Gets Tested on AP Exams Gets Taught in AP Courses

APUSH is "designed to be the equivalent of a two-semester introductory college or university U.S. history course."[22] One of the main reasons that students take APUSH is to earn college admission and credit, and the College Board incentivizes students to figure out how to study and employ strategies to get a 4 or 5, the scores that are often sufficient to earn college credit. To understand what students actually learn in APUSH, one ought to bracket the College Board's rhetoric and look at the details of the testing regime. According to the Princeton Review, graders spend approximately two minutes scoring the written components of an APUSH exam; students need to learn the grading template if they are to "crack" the exam.[23]

The APUSH exam is structured as follows. Section I includes multiple-choice questions (40 percent of total exam score) and short-answer essays (20 percent). Next is a fifteen-minute reading period. Section II includes an essay on a document-based question (25 percent) and a long essay (15 percent). My main source for the exam and strategies for how to score well on it is The Princeton Review's *Cracking the AP U.S. History Exam 2017 Edition,* which includes two practice tests.

Here is an example from the multiple-choice section that lasts fifty-five minutes. Questions 1–4 refer to excerpts about human rights in Latin America. Question 4 asks: "Maize cultivation among the native peoples of Mexico is most analogous to which of the following? (A) Buffalo hunting among the Lakota Sioux (B) Wolf domestication by the Algonquians (C) Mixed agriculture among the Iroquois (D) Seal hunting among the Inuit." In its advice on how to answer the question, the Princeton Review explains how one may answer the question correctly even with no specific knowledge about the native peoples. "Buffalo and seal hunting would require some degree of migration, so rule out (A) and (D), while (B) wolf domestication, would not provide a steady supply of food." Thus, students may deduce that the correct answer is (C). Princeton Review is a different entity than the College Board, but Princeton Review has a granular understanding of the AP program and a track record of preparing students to do well on the AP tests. Their advice is that "even if you cannot remember the specific event or concept being tested, you should be able to answer the question by remembering the general social and political trends of the era and using the information that may be ascertained from the source."[24]

The short-essay section has four questions, each with several parts, and takes fifty minutes. Question 3 is based on an image that the Princeton Review says, in their explanation of the answer, is Theodor de Bry's 1634 painting, "English Trade with Indians." The first part of the question asks the student to "explain the point of view in the image regarding ONE of the following: Commerce, American Indians, European exploration." The rest of the question asks students to identify elements in the painting that express that point of view and how that point of view helped shape significant historical events prior to 1754. The Princeton Review suggests that students identify "European biases about Native Americans in this drawing" and counsels: "Don't worry too much about the picture-based short essay. It tends to allow you to create your own interpretations. Fit your points to your knowledge. Let your imagination be your guide!"[25]

For the moment, I bracket the observation that much of the practice test seems to express a liberal outlook that would probably irritate the conservative signatories of the 2014 Letter. Instead, I want to address the Princeton Review's claim that "excelling on the

AP U.S. History Exam requires a thorough knowledge of the events of American history and their significance."[26] My response is that students do not so much need to know thoroughly American history as to memorize a body of facts and dates provided by the College Board and Princeton Review.

The College Board provides students with a breakdown of what historical periods will be tested on the AP exam. For instance, 5 percent of the AP exam will be on events in the years 1491–1607, while 45 percent will be on the years 1865–1980. The framework lists twenty-eight historical topics, such as World War II and the Turbulent Sixties, that may be covered on the APUSH exam. The framework and the Princeton Review both give detailed guidance on what kind of evidence graders are looking for. For instance, the Princeton Review book has three pages on foreign policy leading up to World War II, and each paragraph uses bold font for concepts such as the Kellogg-Briand Pact and the Good Neighbor Policy. According to the Princeton Review, "If you are familiar with everything in this review, you should do very well on the AP exam."[27]

The APUSH test is eminently test-preppable.

Consider the document-based question, for which students have a suggested reading period of fifteen minutes and a suggested writing period of forty minutes. The test provides excerpts from seven historical documents. The test I took asked a question about the US policy of neutrality during World War I and included passages from letters from President Woodrow Wilson, letters from secretaries of state between 1914 and 1917, stories from the *New York Times*, and so forth. I found the test an interesting intellectual exercise— but there was no pressure on me to get a high score. If students want to achieve a score of 5 on the test, they ought to master the guidelines presented in the College Board's "Rubrics for AP Histories." The rubric specifies how students may earn the seven total possible points. For instance, students earn one point if they present a thesis that makes a "historically defensible claim and responds to all parts of the question," another point if they utilize the content "of at least six of the documents to support the stated thesis," another point if they provide a "piece of specific evidence beyond those found in the documents," and so forth. The Princeton Review adds more advice, including this: "Your first paragraph should contain your thesis statement as the last sentence. Your second, third, and fourth paragraphs should contain three arguments that support that statement, along with historical evidence to back those arguments. The fifth paragraph should state your conclusion, and you must specifically answer the question here."[28] If students learn the rubric, the test-taking strategies, and a few facts about the tested historical eras—pages 276–278 of the Princeton Review book cover US entry into World War I—then they should score well.

The last part of the APUSH test is a long essay question with a suggested writing period of thirty-five minutes. The practice test asks students to write either about the colonists' relationship to British imperial authority leading up to the American Revolution or how the events of the 1960s represented change or continuity over time. Again, the AP testing rubric and the Princeton Review tell students how to structure their essay and what kind of evidence to include. According to the College Board, "To fully and effectively substantiate the stated thesis or a relevant argument, responses must include a broad range of evidence that, through analysis and explanation, justifies the stated thesis or a relevant argument."[29] According to the Princeton Review, "Readers cannot look for anything profound or subtle. What they can do is look for evidence that you have something reasonably intelligent to say and that you know how to say it."[30]

This section has risked stating the obvious: the APUSH test assesses whether students have studied for the APUSH test. In the next two sections, I will explain why this is a problem for democracy.

Protecting the Brand

In the fall of 2014, Jefferson County, Colorado, witnessed a battle over the teaching of US history. Julie Williams, a school board member, proposed to establish a board committee to review the APUSH curriculum framework. Her resolution stated that APUSH "should promote citizenship, patriotism, essentials and benefits of the free enterprise system, respect for authority and respect for individual rights." Honors history courses "should not encourage or condone civil disorder, social strife or disregard of the law"; instead, instructional materials "should present positive aspects of the United States and its heritage."[31]

Students, teachers, and people on Twitter challenged this resolution. Hundreds of students in Jefferson County walked out of class, joined demonstrations and marches, and chanted: "It's our history, don't make it mystery!" Teachers called in sick and used personal days en masse, leading to the closing of at least two schools.[32] On Twitter, people mocked #JeffcoSchoolBoardHistory for supposedly holding that "Pearl Harbor was attacked by Iraqis who snuck across the Mexican border" and "If only Rosa Parks followed orders & sat where she was supposed to, Bengazi never would have happened." One person tweeted: "This #JeffcoSchoolBoardHistory thread is hilarious. Wait a minute . . . my kids are in JeffCo schools. Not so funny."[33]

For its part, the College Board criticized the Jefferson County school board for censorship and misunderstanding how the Advanced Placement program works. "The College Board's Advanced Placement Program supports the actions taken by students in Jefferson County, Colorado to protest a school board member's request to censor aspects of the AP U.S. History course. . . . These students recognize that the social order can—and sometimes must—be disrupted in the pursuit of liberty and justice." In addition, and more concretely, "To offer a course labeled 'AP' or 'Advanced Placement,' a school must agree to meet the expectations set for such courses by the more than 3,300 colleges and universities across the globe that use AP Exam scores for credit, placement, or consideration in the admission process."[34] The College Board framed the Jefferson County APUSH battle as one between enlightened academics and provincial rubes, and given that the three conservative school board members lost their election campaigns in the fall of 2015, the College Board apparently won the battle of ideas.[35]

Another side to the story is that the College Board is protecting its brand, a de facto monopoly on college credit–bearing high school courses.

The College Board stipulates the courses must pass the AP Course Audit to be designated as AP. "Participation in the AP Course Audit requires the online submission of two documents: the AP Course Audit form and the teacher's syllabus. The AP Course Audit form is submitted by the AP teacher and the school principal (or designated administrator) to confirm awareness and understanding of the curricular and resource requirements."[36] The College Board provides annotated sample syllabi, information about curricular and resource requirements, a list of suitable textbooks, a guide to develop syllabi, and a tutorial to help courses pass the audit.[37] The College Board, not local education authorities, decides whether a syllabus, textbook, or curricular resources satisfy AP criteria.

In an article in the *National Review*, Frederick M. Hess and Max Eden argue that conservatives may stop fighting the College Board because the 2015 APUSH framework is "scrupulously fair-minded." Their article details how the new framework provides, from a conservative point of view, a more balanced account of the Declaration of Independence, World War II, and Presidents Franklin Roosevelt and Ronald Reagan. "Faced with a barrage of well-deserved criticism, the College Board went back to the drawing board. It has returned with a framework that offers an honest, fair-minded framework for teaching the grand sweep of American history."[38] In response to criticism, the College Board hired Jeremy Stern, an education consultant with the Thomas B. Fordham Institute, to provide a more balanced account of US history.[39] As Eden details in an American Enterprise Institute report called "The Mend of History," the 2015 framework reflects the values of "well-informed citizens" rather than "denizens of academia."[40]

In a *National Review* article posted on the same day, Stanley Kurtz replied that the College Board had not addressed the conservative critique. "Since the College Board has said that the revised framework will not require modifications to textbooks, there is reason to believe that we are looking at largely cosmetic changes." Furthermore, Kurtz noted that the revised framework uses some conservative buzzwords without incorporating a true conservative outlook. "While the College Board has added a theme on 'American and National Identity'—and even briefly used the phrase 'American Exceptionalism'—I've so far seen little new substance to fill out the meaning of that theme. There is still no treatment of John Winthrop's City on a Hill speech, or of the broader point that the New England settlers saw their venture as a model for the world. . . . Merely referencing the words 'American exceptionalism' isn't enough. To be meaningful, the concept has to be filled out with powerful examples."[41]

According to Kurtz, the College Board needs a conservative competitor: "The only real solution is to nurture competition in AP testing. Whatever limited improvement we're now seeing is due to the specter of competition. Only competition in AP testing can restore choice to the states and school districts that by rights ought to control their own curricula. Without competition, whatever the College Board says, goes."[42]

The Politics of Storytelling

I am sympathetic to the teachers and students who marched in Jefferson County, Colorado, to protest the school board's plans to teach a version of history that extols authority, patriotism, and the free market. At the same time, I would have counseled the protesters that they should not, in effect, give the College Board a blank check to write a detailed, prescriptive curriculum framework for nearly all college credit–bearing high school US history courses. The principle of local control worked in Jefferson County when the conservative school board members were defeated. In *The Human Condition*, the German-Jewish political theorist Hannah Arendt provides insight on why communities ought to debate and decide among themselves about how to teach history.

For Arendt, historians play a crucial role in preserving a community's memory of political action. "Action reveals itself fully only to the storyteller, that is, to the backward glance of the historian."[43] History is what ensures that a community remembers the great words and great deeds of its political actors. Arendt's examples are primarily from Greek and Roman antiquity, but one can recall instances where histories frame our collective memory of prominent political actors. By deciding whom to remember, celebrate, or condemn, or what events shaped our fate, we decide who we are as a political community.

Who should write history? What is the relevant community that decides what political actors to celebrate and which ones to drift off into oblivion? Arendt leaves this an open question in *The Human Condition*, but she gives us a clue for the American context in her 1959 essay, "Reflections on Little Rock." Here, Arendt explains, "states' rights in this country are among the most authentic sources of power, not only for the promotion of regional interests and diversity, but for the Republic as a whole." Given that the federal government had just sent troops to desegregate the Little Rock public schools, Arendt's position made her a lightning rod for criticism. She asks readers not to assume that she is a racist: "I should like to make it clear that as a Jew I take my sympathy for the cause of the Negroes as for all oppressed or underprivileged peoples for granted." Rather, Arendt's argument is that "liberals fail to understand that the nature of power is such that the power potential of the Union as a whole will suffer if the regional foundations on which this power rests are undermined."[44] In other words, Arendt thinks that liberals make a mistake to assume that centralized power will always be smart and enlightened and decentralized power will always be ignorant and racist. The danger is that trusting the capital, or any centralized power, to make important political decisions means that the civic muscle in the provinces will wither.[45]

For Arendt and other democratic political theorists, people may thoughtfully disagree about matters such as how to teach American history and communities should have vibrant debates about what kinds of stories they want to tell about themselves.

The College Board could respond that the curriculum framework provides opportunities for teachers to select the examples of individuals, ideas, and sources to illustrate the key concepts. Conservatives can reply that the rubric frames the issue in a certain way. For example, the 1865–1898 unit asks teachers to provide examples of when "business leaders sought increased profits by consolidating corporations into large trusts and holding companies, which further concentrated wealth."[46] Conservatives could say that this standard presents corporations in a negative light and neglects how big business provides affordable food, housing, and clothing to more and more people. The framework invites teachers to provide examples, from 1844–1877, of how "segregation, violence, Supreme Court decisions, and local political tactics progressively stripped away African American rights" and how the "14th and 15th amendments eventually became the basis for court decisions upholding civil rights in the 20th century."[47] The framework celebrates the federal government and Supreme Court for rectifying racial injustice, neglecting, for instance, to mention how economists such as Gary Becker provided a different set of reasons at the time for why people should oppose segregation. In addition, the College Board released the 2016 APUSH exam, and the free-response question asks students to "explain the causes of the rise of a women's rights movement in the period 1940–1975." Source documents include an essay by Betty Friedan, a press release from New York Radical Women, and a document called "Women: New Voice of La Raza."[48] Conservatives could, with justification, think that the College Board is pushing an anti-business, pro-government ideology in line with radical feminism. Even if one agrees with this ideology, democrats should see a problem with one organization having an outsized power to impart the country's history to young people.

Conclusion

In 1917, one year after writing *Democracy and Education*, John Dewey published an essay called "The Principle of Nationality." He wrote, "Variety *is* the spice of life, and the richness and attractiveness of social institutions depend upon cultural diversity among separate units. . . . The United States is very much more interesting and more promising a place just because there is so much local diversity, because the people of the South are different than the people of New England, and Middle Westerners are different from Far Westerners. Each of these separate localities has its own diversifications to contribute to American life."[49] This statement contains an insight that courses through this entire book, particularly regarding the teaching of US history.

Democrats should empower local communities to decide their standards for the teaching and learning of history. In New York, we may emphasize the role that journalists, financiers, and artists have played in American history; in the Midwest, local education authorities may accentuate the role played by farmers and industrialists; in California, schools may concentrate on agriculture and the entertainment industry; and Hawaii may concentrate on the history of the islands in ways that would not interest students in Maine. Different communities may choose different political actors to remember, and these debates over history can be a way to practice what Arendt calls the *vita activa*. Elite private schools have already started to exit the AP program and design their own history courses, and democrats should encourage this process to take place throughout the country.

Many outstanding schools and teachers participate in the AP program, but they are being stifled by a curriculum framework that has an ideological bias and a focus on test preparation. The country needs to break the College Board's monopoly on honors US history courses and create conditions for many people to have a meaningful say in how young people learn history.

SEVEN

Sexuality Standards, Gender Identity, and Religious Minorities

T his chapter discusses the National Sexuality Education Standards (NSES), beginning with an explanation of the history and guiding values of the standards, followed by a focus on one of the more controversial features of the NSES—the treatment of gender identity—and the lesson plans for this topic in a textbook. Liberal democracy requires a balance between the rule of the majority and protection of minority rights, and religious minorities may view the NSES as imposing values on an area that is the parents' prerogative. To illustrate this point, I show how Muslims may object to certain features of the NSES, including its coverage of gender identity. Given that reasonable people disagree about the content of sexuality education standards, pluralistic democracies should permit communities to choose their own sexuality education standards with exit options for families.

The History of the Sexuality Education Standards

In 2012, the *American Journal of Health Education* published a special supplement called "National Sexuality Education Standards: Core Content and Skills, K–12," which stated that the goal of NSES is to provide "clear, consistent and straightforward guidance on the essential minimum, core content for sexuality education that is developmentally and age-appropriate for students in grades K–12."[1]

Three sexual education organizations—Advocates for Youth, Answer, and Sexuality Information and Education Council of the U.S. (SIECUS)—collaborated on the Future of Sex Education Initiative (FoSE) to write and promote the NSES as a way to structure comprehensive sexuality education courses throughout the country.[2] In December 2008, FoSE organized a two-day meeting of forty individuals from the fields of health education, sexuality education, public health, public policy, philanthropy, and advocacy to create a strategic plan for sexuality education policy. This meeting led to the writing of the NSES, building upon the foundation of the National Health Education Standards (NHES) that were created by the Joint Committee on National Health Education Standards of the American Cancer Society in 1995 and modified in 2007. The four official FoSE partners in designing the NSES were the American Association for Health Education, the American School Health Association, the National Education Association—Health Information Network, and the Society of State Leaders of Health and Physical Education. The goal of the NSES is to modernize sexual health education in our country, preferably with the help of the federal government.[3]

Up to now, the NSES has not transformed the public school curriculum to the same degree as the other standards we have considered in this book. Powerful constituencies, however, support the NSES, including state boards of education, the Centers for Disease Control, the Council of Chief State School Officers, and the National Association of State Boards of Education. And if schools of education adopt the "National Teacher Preparation Standards for Sexuality Education," then the NSES may become the de facto national sexuality education standards.[4]

The Common Core State Standards for ELA and Mathematics served as a model for the NSES.[5] While the Gates Foundation has not contributed to FoSE, funders of the NSES include the Ford Foundation, the George Gund Foundation, and the Grove Foundation.[6] The architects or lead writers of the Common Core standards did not write the NSES. Instead, organizations such as SIECUS—founded in 1964 by Mary Calderone, medical director at Planned

Parenthood—think that the Common Core State Standards Initiative illustrates a way to enact systemic education reform in sexuality education. National sexuality education standards may "provide a framework for curriculum development, instruction and student assessment," "reflect the research-based characteristics of effective sexuality education," "teach functional knowledge and essential personal and social skills that contribute directly to healthy sexuality," "consider the developmental appropriateness of material for students in specific grade spans," and "include a progression from more concrete to higher-order thinking skills."[7]

The Philosophy of the National Sexuality Education Standards

According to the NSES document, the United States has one of the highest teen pregnancy rates in the industrialized world; many young women have unintended pregnancies; young people ages 15–25 contract about half of the nineteen million sexually transmitted diseases (STDs) annually, including HIV. Furthermore, there is "a pressing need to address harassment, bullying and relationship violence in our schools, which have a significant impact on a student's emotional and physical well-being as well as on academic success. According to the 2009 National School Climate Survey, nearly 9 out of 10 lesbian, gay, bisexual or transgender (LGBT) students reported being harassed in the previous year."[8]

In a commentary in *Education Week*, Debra Hauser, president of Advocates for Youth, Monica Rodriquez, president of SIECUS, Elizabeth Schroeder, executive director of Answer, and Danene Sorace, a consultant for FoSE, explain that the NSES "provide nonbinding guidelines for the minimum content young people need to receive in sexuality education in kindergarten through 12th grade. They are based on scientific evidence, child and adolescent development, and learning theory, and outline the information and skills that research tells us students need to acquire by each grade."[9] The guiding values of the NSES are that "all students, regardless of physical or intellectual ability, deserve the opportunity to achieve personal health and wellness, including sexual health" and "sexuality education should teach both information and essential skills that are necessary to adopt, practice, and maintain healthy relationships and behaviors."[10]

Philosophers sometimes distinguish "concepts" from "conceptions"—that is, general notions that most people endorse as opposed to fleshed-out versions that are often a subject of disagreement. It would be hard to find parents or educators opposed to the concept of "personal health and wellness." But what is the NSES's conception of sexual education?

The NSES presents the standards by grade levels K–2, 3–5, 6–8, and 9–12. For each grade band, students study seven topics and eight National Health Education Standards (NHES). The seven topics include Anatomy and Physiology (AP), Puberty and Adolescent Development (PD), Identity (ID), Pregnancy and Reproduction (PR), Sexually Transmitted Diseases and HIV (SH), Healthy Relationships (HR), and Personal Safety (PS). The eight NHES standards start with Core Concepts (CC) and then proceed to identify actions including Analyzing Influences (INF), Accessing Information (AI), Interpersonal Communication (IC), Decision-Making (DM), Goal-Setting (GM), Self Management (SM), and Advocacy (ADV).

According to the NSES standards for the Core Concepts for Identity, for example, by the end of second grade students should be able to "describe differences and similarities in how boys and girls may be expected to act"; by the end of fifth grade, "define sexual orientation as the romantic attraction of an individual to someone of the same gender or a different gender"; by the end of eighth grade, "differentiate between gender identity, gender expression and sexual orientation" and "explain the range of gender roles"; and by the end of twelfth grade, "differentiate between biological sex, sexual orientation, and gender identity and expression" and "distinguish between sexual orientation, sexual behavior and sexual identity."[11]

The NSES standards for the Core Concepts for Pregnancy and Reproduction state that by the end of second grade, students should be able to "explain that all living things reproduce"; by the end of fifth grade, "describe the process of human reproduction"; by the end of eighth grade, "define sexual intercourse and its relationship to human reproduction," "define sexual abstinence as it relates to pregnancy prevention," "explain the health benefits, risks and effectiveness rates of various methods of contraception, including abstinence and condoms," and "define emergency contraception and its use"; and by the end of twelfth grade, "define emergency contraception and describe its mechanism of action" and "identify the laws related to reproductive and sexual health care services (i.e., contraception, pregnancy options, safe surrender policies, prenatal care)."[12]

Identity Bingo

In *Too Hot to Handle*, Jonathan Zimmerman identifies the "Big Four" taboos for sexuality educators around the globe: abortion, contraception, homosexuality, and masturbation.[13] We see this pattern in surveys on American parental attitudes toward school-based sexuality education. For example, a national random sample of parents of elementary school-age children found that 91 percent of parents favored teaching about friendship and bully prevention, but the number dropped to 58 percent in favor of learning about "different kinds of families."[14] Or, a survey of Utah parents of elementary school-age children found support for many of the NSES standards except for three topics that had a greater than 25 percent disapproval rate: teaching how to use a condom; laws and methods relating to abortion; and homosexuality, sexual orientation, and gender identity.[15] A survey at a culturally diverse community college also found near unanimity on the importance of teaching the basics of reproduction and the transmission and prevention of sexually transmitted infections (STIs), while respondents answered that they were opposed to teaching or considered not at all important the following topics: abortion (41 percent), masturbation (57 percent), oral sex (62 percent), anal sex (75 percent), or sexual orientation (33 percent).[16]

To anticipate the political and cultural battles on sexuality education that may be on the horizon, we can refer to a textbook that provides lesson plans to satisfy the NSES. In 2014, Dominick Splendorio and Lori A. Reichel published *Tools for Teaching Comprehensive Human Sexuality Education: Lessons, Activities, and Teaching Strategies Utilizing the National Sexual Education Standards*. The book has seven chapters, one for each topic in the NSES, and each lesson plan identifies the relevant National Health Education Standards, the NSES performance indicators, a rationale, a procedure with an itemized list of activities, questions to facilitate student processing, and assessment guides.

Chapter 3, "Identity," opens by saying that "in every society, gender norms and gender roles influence people's lives, including their sexual lives. Greater equality and more flexible gender roles give all of us more opportunities to develop to our full potential as human beings."[17] The book advises, "Students have the right to their opinions and values, yet need to be respectful of others when sharing them."[18]

Lesson 1, "Identity Bingo," covers the National Health Education Standards of Core Concepts (CC) and Interpersonal Communication (IC) and NSES performance indicators, such as being able to distinguish between sexual orientation, sexual behavior, and sexual identity. The rationale for the lesson is that "terms used within sexual identity lessons are often misunderstood and misused." Therefore, "this lesson reviews the appropriate terms and their definitions so that students will come to understand what terminology is appropriate when discussing sexual identity."[19]

How does the game work? The teacher distributes to the students blank bingo worksheets with five columns, five rows, and a free space in the center. The students fill in each square using a list of terms that includes the following: female, male, GLBTQ, heterosexual, bisexual, transvestite, heterosexism, respect, advocacy, transgender, and gay. Then, the teacher reads definitions aloud, and if the students find the matching word, they check the appropriate square. The normal bingo rules apply to the rest of the game, though the lesson plan directs the teacher to conclude by discussing the following statements: "Almost everything males can do, females can do. Almost everything females can do, males can do."[20]

Among the definitions teachers use in the bingo game are these. Gender identity is "a person's inner sense of being male or female, resulting from a combination of genetic and environmental influences." Homophobia is "the fear or hatred of someone who identifies as gay, lesbian, bisexual, or transgender." A homosexual is "a person who is attracted to a person of the same sex."[21] The lesson plan includes the following note: "Because the topic of gender roles and sexual orientation may make some students uncomfortable, plan ways to diffuse potential disagreements and maintain open and respectful discussion. As always, students have the right to their opinions."[22]

That is not exactly true: students may have a right to their opinions, but the assessment portion of the lesson plan states that students must "complete the bingo game, recognizing each term's proper use and definition." Additionally, students get points for their participation. If a student has a "pleasant facial expression," they get full points, but if they have "tense muscles" and a "scowl on face," then they get no points.[23] Students who are visibly discomfited by the materials will receive a lower grade.

When I first taught the NSES in an honors seminar at Fordham University, virtually all of the students thought that it was appropriate for sexuality education classes to teach about gender identity and various forms of contraception and abortion. Nearly all western sex educators believe that it is good science and good ethics to teach children to respect homosexuals and the right to an abortion. And there are political theorists who think that schools may and should teach children about the range of human sexuality and the need to tolerate other ways of life. Still, this lesson plan confirms the suspicion that the NSES could be used to teach government-sanctioned views of sexual ethics. Even if one agrees with the definitions, democrats ought to be uncomfortable with schools teaching such sensitive material in a way that many citizens oppose. I elaborate this point in the next section by considering a Muslim perspective on comprehensive sexuality education.

Sexuality Education and Religious Minorities

Liberal democracy combines majority rule and minority rights. Democracy means rule by the people, but few political theorists today equate democracy with majoritarianism, the idea that a bare majority ought to get its way in all cases. The American constitutional framework, for instance, gives voters the right to elect representatives, but then places boundaries on majority rule, including judicial review of legislation, the need for supermajorities on certain issues, and federalism, a division of power between federal, state, and local governments. Saying that 51 percent of the country favors the teaching of a topic in school is just one datum in a democratic conversation about the curriculum.

According to Jonathan Zimmerman in *Too Hot to Handle*, the history of sex education in the past century has been a struggle between western sex educators and conservatives around the globe. The former tend to celebrate the power of the individual to make important decisions about sex, and the latter tend to think that sexual autonomy is a recipe for vice, individual tragedy, and community disintegration. "Examine almost any sex education document— in almost any part of the globe—and you will find statements exalting the conscience and choice of the rational individual. . . . To many people around the world, however, that idea offends *their* conscience; they want schools to map proper sexual behavior, not to liberate individuals to explore it on their own."[24] In the United States, for instance, Valerie Huber of Ascend—formerly the National Abstinence Education Association—criticizes the NSES and comprehensive sexuality education in general for normalizing teen sex.[25]

At least since the Scopes Trial of 1925, many American liberals tend to dismiss the concerns of Christian fundamentalists as being based on superstition rather than science.[26] As noted in the last section, many sex educators, college students, and liberal political theorists seem ready to combat Christian fundamentalists on the terrain of sexuality education. Might the conversation shift if we bring in other religious constituencies that oppose comprehensive sexuality education? Might liberals be more receptive to religious critiques if they are not made by a historical antagonist in American politics? I pursue that intimation in this section by considering how many Muslims reject the values and principles of comprehensive sexuality education.

In a 1998 article in the *Cambridge Journal of Education*, "Should Homosexuality Be Taught as an Acceptable Alternative Lifestyle? A Muslim Perspective," J. Mark Halstead and Katarzyna Lewicka argue that many Muslims object to at least two aspects of western comprehensive sexuality education. First, Muslims oppose homosexuality as a forbidden (*haram*) act. The most common Arabic term for homosexuality, *liwat*, alludes to the sexual behavior of the people with whom the prophet Lot lived. There are Prophetic sayings (*hadith*) that specify that both the active and the passive participants in a homosexual relationship must be killed. Homosexuality "is condemned because it involves the rebellious rejection of the harmonious complementarity of the sexes which God has ordained."[27] Halstead and Lewicka acknowledge that Muslims have a wide diversity of practice in regard to homosexuality and that they rarely enforce the death penalty on homosexuals. When they do—say, in Iran in the 1980s—there are often other factors at work, such as anti-western sentiment. That said, Muslim jurists or scholars rarely doubt that divine law (sharia) forbids homosexual acts.

Furthermore, according to Halstead and Lewicka, Muslims think in terms of acts, not inclinations or orientations. Islam enjoins Muslims to do the good and forbid the evil. "Islam teaches that if people have sinful desires they should keep to themselves and control them in order to avoid doing what God has forbidden."[28]

Muslims should not tolerate forbidden behavior; they have a moral responsibility to encourage the person to "get back on the right path."[29]

Is Islam homophobic? Halstead and Lewicka think that this is the wrong way to frame the question. "Muslims do not *fear* homosexuality, they *disapprove* of it."[30] Halstead and Lewicka identify assumptions that many western homosexuals take for granted, including that sexual orientation is not a choice, that homosexuality and heterosexuality are equally natural, and that "*all* pupils need to be presented with balanced and accurate information about sexual identity and sexual orientation, so that irrational fear and prejudice can be challenged and pupils can come to see homosexuality as a normal and acceptable lifestyle."[31] Most Muslims think that the relevant ethical and legal criterion is action, that sharia prohibits homosexuality, and that there is no obligation on Muslims to tolerate homosexuality as an ethical practice. "From an Islamic point of view it makes no more sense to say one has been 'created homosexual' than it does to say one has been 'created adulterous'; both involve intentional actions which contravene God's law."[32]

Sex educators, according to Halstead and Lewicka, should teach Muslims certain topics only after they have already been socialized as Muslims. Experts in sexuality education should not try to convert Muslims nor "promote the lesbian and gay perspective uncritically in their publications." The reason is that society should "enable different minority communities with different values and ways of understanding the world to live together in harmony and to enable each in their different ways to contribute to the well-being of the broader society."[33]

Michael S. Merry criticizes Halstead and Lewicka for ignoring Islamic sources for comprehensive sexuality education, neglecting gay and lesbian Muslims who may be persecuted, and placing restrictions on what sex educators may do to facilitate positive encounters between homosexuals and Muslims in the classroom.[34]

In reply, Halstead argues that sexuality educators can perpetrate cultural imperialism if they condescend to religious believers or offer simplistic reinterpretations favorable to gay rights. Halstead envisions a certain principle of reciprocity between Muslims and homosexuals who simply proceed from different assumptions. "It should be possible for Muslims to set out a religious perspective that is critical of homosexual behavior without being accused of homophobia, just as it is possible for homosexuals to criticize Islamic teaching about sexual behavior without being accused of Islamophobia."[35] Halstead treads carefully because he knows that many western sexuality educators think that this perspective is beyond the pale. Halstead is not a Muslim nor does he advocate anything like cruelty toward homosexuals. Instead, he argues that sexuality educators ought to be more critical of their own assumptions when communicating with people of different religious traditions. "If real dialogue is to take place between homosexuals and Muslims, there has to be a willingness for each party to listen to and engage with the actual beliefs and worldviews of the other, however unpalatable these may be at first sight."[36]

Is the conflict between Islam and comprehensive sexuality education insurmountable? HEART Women and Girls, founded by Nadiah Mohajir and Ayesha Akhtar, advocates "sexual and reproductive health programming for Muslim American youth that is engaging, accurate, relatable, and most importantly, in line with Islamic values."[37] On the one hand, the HEART Women and Girls documents align with the scholarly literature on comprehensive sexuality education. One of the funders of the organization is the Muslim Youth Project at Advocates for Youth, and its literature cites the NSES. On the other hand, the HEART Women and Girls literature works within the Islamic tradition and its concepts such as *haya* (modesty) and *amana* (trust). HEART Women and Girls documents cite sayings (hadith) of the Prophet Muhammad to his Companions instructing them to learn about their bodies as well as al-Ghazali's teaching that Muslims must protect their physical, emotional, and spiritual health.[38] HEART Women and Girls acknowledges Halstead's critique of western sexuality education but does not think that this ends the conversation: Muslim women can get pregnant, be abused, or learn about sexuality through pornography just as other women do, and it is important that they learn the facts of life.

The HEART Women and Girls guide to educating Muslim youth, however, does not touch perhaps the most controversial topic of the NSES: gender identity. The guide acknowledges, "Some of the language used in this toolkit may sound exclusive, particularly to the Lesbian, Gay, Bisexual, Transgender, and Queer (LGBTQ) community. The Muslim LGBTQ community is growing, and Muslims must address the concerns of this community. As such, this toolkit cannot do justice to addressing all of the complex issues pertaining to sexuality, sexual orientation, gender identity and Islam."[39] For a document that mentions Halstead by name, lists his arguments, and warns against Muslim sexuality educators placing too many constraints on themselves, it is noteworthy that HEART Women and Girls provides minimal guidance on how to educate gay Muslim youth or teach Muslim youth about homosexuality.

In *Too Hot to Handle*, Zimmerman notes that western sexual educators often get a chilly reception while traveling overseas. Religious conservatives around the world defend traditional notions of sexual morality, and liberals struggle "to respect ethnic and religious 'diversity' " even as they proclaim "a universal right to sexual choice and information."[40] We can anticipate that dynamic at work if the NSES standards are used in classes with Muslim students.

Conclusion

I doubt that it is possible to create national sexuality education standards that will satisfy all factions in American politics. Nancy Kendall provides evidence for this thesis in her book, *The Sex Education Debates*. On the one hand, Abstinence Only Until Marriage Education (AOUME) proponents argue that sex is "private and sacred and that abstinence is the only morally correct option for unmarried people."[41] To its critics, however, the abstinence-only agenda expresses cruelty toward people who do not fit its heteronormative, middle-class, and implicitly Christian agenda. On the other hand, advocates of Comprehensive Sexuality Education (CSE) claim to base their views on objective, value-free science, but they often use moral terms to criticize traditional perspectives and ignore scientific evidence that undermines their claims—for instance, claims about the potential benefits of teen versus later pregnancy.[42] Kendall envisions a democratic conception of sexuality education that synthesizes both major camps. As interesting as this thought experiment may be, however, this solution will likely not work. For instance, she suggests that a unit on the Internet and sexuality might "talk about the Internet and pornography" and "visit popular teen chat rooms."[43] For many conservatives, a problem with comprehensive sexuality education is that it teaches students about things that they should not do. Researching pornography on the Internet seems like a case in point.

For comprehensive sex educators, however, the importance of the issues—such as HIV, STIs, teen pregnancy, or bullying—demands that schools teach what works. The NSES states that comprehensive sexuality education programs "can help youth delay the onset of sexual activity, reduce the frequency of sexual activity, reduce the number of sexual partners, and increase condom and contraceptive use."[44] The citation, however, is to a report from Advocates from Youth, one of the groups that created the NSES. A more honest assessment is from an article that generally supports the NSES but acknowledges, "the NSES are not empirically validated" and have "not been translated into a curriculum that has produced evidence in achieving specific health outcomes."[45] Furthermore, there are reasons to be skeptical about the efficacy of the NSES: "Scholars around the world have struggled in vain to show *any* significant influence of sex education upon youth sexual behavior."[46] One might even anticipate that certain NSES-aligned lesson plans—such as Identity Bingo—could backfire in certain circumstances.

So what should be done in regard to sexuality education? One possibility is that schools avoid sexuality education and instead concentrate on academic subjects such as ELA and math. That is arguably what has happened across the country in the era of standards-based education reform.[47] But the main argument of this book is that democracy entails empowering communities to have a say over the curriculum, and if a community wants to cover sexuality education, then that should be its prerogative. At the same time, democrats should be wary of thinking that one set of sexuality standards can possibly satisfy all or even most Americans. Many advocates of the NSES seem to assume that LGBTQ-friendly people will be in charge of the project to nationalize sexuality education, but that may not always be the case. US President Donald Trump appointed Betsy DeVos as Secretary of Education, and the DeVos family has a history of combating the gay rights movement and funding groups that support gay conversion.[48] The LGBTQ community would likely oppose any conception of national sexuality education standards that she supports.

Rather than fight this battle on a national stage, then, Americans should preserve our constitutional framework that assigns the power of education to the states and that grants exit rights to individuals. There is no reason that New York and Utah must adopt the same set of sexuality education standards that inevitably express a moral worldview. Given the diversity within states, I would go even further and argue for the democratic benefits of entrusting local communities to decide their own sexuality education standards. Fredonia, a more conservative city in upstate New York, should not necessarily have the same sexuality education standards as Brooklyn, one of the most liberal parts of the country. But doesn't this position risk exposing gay children to the mercy of intolerant communities? It bears repeating that the NSES has no proven track record, and it is also possible that the people who believe in gay conversion could be in charge of formulating national sexuality education standards. In a Trump administration, do liberals really want to say that sexuality education is a national issue? And if and when the tables turn, might liberals see the value of exercising restraint and not resuming the project of nationalizing a single vision of sexual health?

National sexuality education standards are a powerful tool to influence the teaching of sexual health, gender identities, personal responsibility, and numerous other important and controversial topics. At the same time, if the NSES were to become more widely adopted, then many families would be furious that the schools were teaching children things that they oppose. Families would be disenfranchised from one of the most important decisions that they make about how to raise their own children. There is no need to settle the cultural wars in this manner. Let communities debate what they want to teach children about sexuality. Let parents pull their children from lessons that violate their religious and ethical beliefs. And let the battle about sexual education continue on multiple fronts without any one faction using the nuclear weapon of national standards.

Democracy, Education Standards, and Local Control

....

On September 27 and 28, 1989, President George H. W. Bush and forty-nine governors met at the University of Virginia and announced that the country needed to set national education goals, use federal resources to meet those goals, and undertake a state-by-state effort to create a national education system. Over the next few decades, people at that meeting would take the lead in writing legislation, implementing policy, and promoting national education standards. According to Thomas H. Kean, who served as Republican governor of New Jersey at the time, "the Common Core is a descendant" of Charlottesville.[1] From one perspective, the Common Core lost, because many states have revised and renamed the standards. From another, the Common Core won, because most states as of 2017 have retained the ELA and math standards and "clarified wording without changing content."[2] Multiple factors, including Common Core–aligned college entrance exams, make it difficult for states, cities, or even homeschooling families to avoid the Common Core.[3] Many states have adopted the Next Generation Science Standards, and schools throughout the country use the Advanced Placement U.S. History Course (APUSH) curriculum framework. If the National Sexuality Education Standards transform teacher training, then they may become the country's de facto national standards.

People have protested each set of standards. Progressives object to the Common Core's focus on close reading that demands that children "quote accurately" from the text, rather than share their own thoughts, to earn full credit on assignments or assessments. Traditionalists argue that the Common Core's emphasis on showing your work in math sets up a roadblock to children on the autism spectrum who might otherwise become outstanding mathematicians. Critics of the Next Generation Science Standards argue that the standards' treatment of sustainability places too much trust in technological fixes rather than hard political choices. Conservatives argue that the APUSH curriculum framework presents a self-hating view of American identity, and the National Sexuality Education Standards' view of gender identity contravenes the way many Muslims view the topic. In the language of Federalist 10, one faction has determined how most American schools teach English, math, science, honors history, and sexuality education, and other factions have almost no recourse within public education. The long-term effect is to alienate many Americans from public education and civic life in general.[4]

This conclusion envisions an alternative to national education standards and a path to create a more democratic and diverse educational landscape.

Initially, I explain how the federal government has used Title I of the Elementary and Secondary Education Act (ESEA) to pressure states to adopt certain education standards. Then, I explain how the 2015 ESEA reauthorization, the Every Student Succeeds Act (ESSA), requires states and local education authorities to combat the opt-out movement, one of the main ways that families have signaled disapproval of standards-based education reform. Some scholars contend that a new accountability paradigm may mitigate problems with standards-based reform such as a narrowing of the curriculum; I argue that the proposed solutions do not sufficiently address the democratic critique of national education standards. I reconstruct John Dewey's arguments for why we ought to create an education system that empowers communities, teachers, and students to make or select educational standards. The federal government may redistribute resources to ensure that all children receive a quality education, but democracy requires ordinary people to have a say over the local schools' philosophy of education. One way out of our predicament may be a return to the original ESEA's framework of equitably distributing financial aid while honoring the rights of communities to determine their own educational priorities. Finally, in response to the equity argument for national education standards, I argue that historically disadvantaged communities, as surely as any other community, ought to have a role in determining the local schools' philosophy of education.

The Federal Government and National Education Standards

Many scholars and policymakers tell a version of the story in which the Elementary and Secondary Education Act has progressed from a weak and compromised civil rights law to one that brings us closer to its latent ideal of equitable and excellent education for all. My goal in this section is to complicate this narrative by showing that the original ESEA has centralizing elements while its subsequent reauthorizations contain decentralizing aspects. One could argue that the history of American political thought tells of an ongoing tug-of-war between Hamiltonian Federalists and Madisonian Democratic Republicans—those who favor a strong federal government and those who wish for states and communities to have more power. There is nothing inevitable about the federal government setting education standards; the question for us is whether to accept or contest this distribution of power.

President Lyndon Johnson viewed ESEA as the cornerstone for his War on Poverty and a way to provide "full educational opportunity" to all American children. Johnson explained, "Our war on poverty can be won only if those who are poverty's prisoners can break the chains of ignorance." After the civil rights movement prompted a national debate on how to achieve racial justice, and President Kennedy's assassination gave LBJ an opportunity to fulfill

Kennedy's civil rights agenda, the new president used his legislative acumen to pass a bill that raised federal spending on education to about $1 billion. Congress wanted to increase funding for areas affected by poverty, and the policy community wanted the federal government to invest in education research and innovation, but the reigning story is that "from its inception, ESEA was a civil rights law."[5]

The Elementary and Secondary Education Act of 1965 contained at least two checks on federal control over the curriculum. First, ESEA was a categorical granting program that required states to design compensatory education programs for students suffering from poverty or the legacy of racism. It was not a block grant that gave states and school districts full discretion over how to spend the money, but neither did it closely regulate how the money should be spent. Title I of ESEA distributed money to most congressional districts and was "designed to keep central authority weak."[6] Furthermore, the law specified that "nothing contained in this Act shall be construed to authorize any department, agency, officer, or employee of the United States to exercise any direction, supervision, or control over the curriculum."[7] Nearly fifty years later, Secretary of Education Arne Duncan reiterated this point when he said that the Common Core is a set of standards, not a curriculum, and that "the federal government didn't write them, didn't approve them, and doesn't mandate them. And we never will."[8] There is a general awareness that the Tenth Amendment of the Constitution prohibits the federal government from writing and testing a uniform curriculum.

Nonetheless, there was pressure even before ESEA passed that the law provide quantitative evidence of academic achievement. During deliberations over Title I in ESEA, Senator Robert F. Kennedy asked "whether it would be possible to have some kind of testing system at the end of a year or 2 years in which we would see whether the money that had been invested in the school district of New York City, or Denver, Colorado, or Jackson, Mississippi, or whatever it might be, was coming up with a plan and program that made it worthwhile, and whether the child, in fact, was gaining from the investment of these funds."[9] His amendment to the law stipulated that "objective measurements of educational achievement" must be collected annually to determine the "effectiveness of the programs" in meeting children's education needs.[10] In the immediate aftermath of ESEA, however, neither Congress nor the president tried to implement this policy.[11] Policymakers in the 1960s knew about the idea of national testing and decided that other factors, including the ideal of federalism and the tradition of local control, were more important.

Initially, ESEA worked primarily in the equity paradigm, whereby policymakers trust educators and communities to spend money responsibly. In the 1960s, schools used Title I funds for state and local priorities such as remedial math and language courses, health and nutritional needs, field trips, band uniforms, and swimming pools.[12] Shortly after ESEA's passage, critics such as sociologist James Coleman argued that educators should be more concerned with outputs, such as higher standardized test scores, than inputs, such as class size or extracurricular options.[13] For advocates of the excellence paradigm, schools should set high academic standards and reward teachers and students who meet them and penalize those who do not. In the 1990s, Democratic legislators argued for "opportunity to learn" standards to complement content and performance standards, but Republicans opposed them, and Democratic leaders such as President Clinton did not push for them.

"A Nation at Risk," published in 1983, hastened the rise of the excellence agenda. This document famously argued that American schools were drowning in a "rising tide of mediocrity" and that the country had been "committing an act of unthinking, unilateral educational disarmament." The report announced that "our goal must be to develop the talents of all to their fullest" and that "we should expect schools to have genuinely high standards rather than minimum ones."[14] "A Nation at Risk" presented low standardized test scores as a national problem; mobilized political actors, including governors and presidents, to address what had long been a local affair;

and shaped how policymakers viewed education reform.[15] Subsequently, policy experts, many of whom participated in the Pew Forum on School Reform based at Stanford University, worked behind the scenes to develop solutions to the problems identified in "A Nation at Risk."[16] These ideas came to the fore with the 1989 education summit; the Goals 2000 law of 1994, which supported the development of state and federal standards and assessments; and the 1994 reauthorization of ESEA, called the Improving America's Schools Act (IASA). The IASA required all states to develop educational standards; assess students at least once in elementary, middle, and high school; and require schools with low test scores to develop an improvement plan. This law marked the first time that the federal government used Title I funds as a means to require states to adopt standards-based reform, though Republican members of Congress gutted the law in 1995.[17]

In 2002, President Bush signed into law No Child Left Behind (NCLB), which pressured states to adopt academic achievement standards, state academic assessments, and accountability systems. "The purpose of this title is to ensure that all children have a fair, equal, and significant opportunity to obtain a high-quality education and reach, at a minimum, proficiency on challenging state academic achievement standards and state academic assessments."[18] States had the prerogative to choose their own academic standards, assessments, and proficiency rates to determine if students were making adequate yearly progress on mastering the state's academic standards. However, the law required all states to test all students in reading and math in grades 3–8 and once in grades 10–12 and to test students in science at least once in elementary, middle, and high school. Schools had to disaggregate testing data for subgroups, including special education, English language learners, racial minorities, and poor children, and if any subgroup did not make adequate yearly progress, the state needed to develop an improvement plan that could eventually lead to the school's becoming a privately managed charter school. If states did not comply with key requirements of NCLB, then they risked losing their administrative allocation from the program; if states did not participate in the standards, testing, and accountability paradigm, then they would be ineligible for Title I funds.[19]

In principle, No Child Left Behind allowed the country to sustain multiple academic standards in reading, math, and science. As I explained in the book's introduction, the Obama administration used the competitive grant program, Race to the Top, to incentivize states to adopt the Common Core standards in ELA and math. Race to the Top did not so much force states to adopt standards against their will as empower constituencies in each state that supported the project of national education standards.

On December 10, 2015, President Obama signed into law the Every Student Succeeds Act (ESSA). According to that law, states must still administer annual statewide assessments of all students' learning, set student performance targets used to rate schools, and intervene in struggling schools as determined primarily by test scores.[20] According to Senator Lamar Alexander (R-TN), the new law signals "the single biggest step toward local control of public schools in 25 years."[21] According to President Obama, however, the new law reaffirms "that fundamentally American ideal—that every child, regardless of race, income, background, the zip code where they live, deserves the chance to make of their lives what they will."[22]

ESSA announces that the federal government will not use Title I funds to influence the standards that states adopt or use: "No officer or employee of the federal government shall, through grants, contracts, or other cooperative agreements, mandate, direct, or control a state, local educational agency, or school's specific instructional content, academic standards and assessments, or program of instruction." More pointedly, the law prohibits the secretary of education from requiring adoption of the Common Core State Standards or putting roadblocks in the way of any state writing new standards.[23]

However, ESSA does specify certain requirements for state academic standards: "Each state shall demonstrate that the challenging state academic standards are aligned with entrance requirements for credit-bearing coursework in the system of public higher education in the state and relevant state career and technical education standards."[24] The law adds, however: "Nothing in this act shall be construed to authorize public institutions of higher education to determine the specific challenging state academic standards."[25] In the fall of 2016, the New York State Education Department held workshops on putting together an ESSA plan and explained that "states need to submit their plans to USDE for review, but states must demonstrate alignment to college and career/technical education standards"—essentially a synonym for the Common Core.[26]

Furthermore, under ESSA the secretary of education must approve a state's education plan to receive Title I funds. ESSA empowers the secretary to decline a state's education plans because of its assessment and accountability components, stating that the secretary will "establish a peer-review process to assist in the review of state plans," and the teams will include "researchers who are familiar with the implementation of academic standards, assessments, or accountability systems." The purpose of peer review is to "promote effective implementation of the challenging state academic standards." If a state's plans do not meet the criteria, "the secretary may withhold funds for state administration under this part until the secretary determines that the state has fulfilled those requirements."[27] Researchers and a secretary of education may approve state plans that include assessments and accountability mechanisms that are unaligned to the Common Core; however, given that the pool of eligible researchers will likely include supporters of the Common Core, states should not assume that approval.

States may retain the Common Core standards because state governments, school administrators, and teachers have spent time, energy, and money adapting to the Common Core. States may also recognize that students should study the Common Core so they will be prepared for the SAT and ACT college entrance exams. But until we see a state choose a substantively different set of academic standards than the Common Core, we may remain skeptical that ESSA represents a sea change in federal education policies regarding standards.[28]

Plans for Test Refusals

In the spring of 2016, hundreds of thousands of American students refused to take the end-of-year Common Core standardized tests.[29] Without this test data, it is difficult to build an accountability system that pressures teachers to teach and students to learn the standards. For many advocates of national education standards, it is essential that the country use comparable tests. How, then, does ESSA address the test refusal movement and its potential to thwart systemic education reform?

As with No Child Left Behind, ESSA requires states to assess students in ELA and mathematics annually in grades 3–8 and once in high school, and assess students in science at least once in elementary, middle, and high school.[30] Under ESSA, states may administer multiple interim tests to create a single summative score. States may also use assessment results from portfolios, projects, or extended performance that meet the standards of psychometric reliability and validity rather than solely multiple-choice standardized tests. ESSA shows how states may undermine the test refusal movement—namely, by eliminating the one big test at the end of the year. But we are not at that moment just yet.

ESSA includes a clause on "parent rights": "Nothing in this [law] shall be construed as preempting a state or local law regarding the decision of a parent to not have the parent's child participate in the academic assessments."[31] A state can pass a law that permits parents to refuse the tests for their children. ESSA, however, requires states to annually measure the achievement of not less than 95 percent of all subgroups, differentiate schools based on participation rate, and use sanctions against schools where the participation rate falls below 95 percent.

This is not an idle threat: ESSA mandates that states identify the worst-performing 5 percent of Title I schools and make them formulate comprehensive support and improvement plans. If schools fail to increase their rate of test participation, they can receive a lower performance rating; if schools do not get a higher rating, then the state can "turn around" the school, including firing the staff and making the school a charter school. In short, communities can lose their school boards; and teachers, principals, and superintendents can lose their jobs if test participation rates are not sufficiently high. In recent years, some administrators have employed the tactic of making test refusing children "sit and stare" while other students take the assessments; this approach could be a prelude to other strategies designed to induce children to take the tests.[32]

In December 2016, the US Department of Education released ESSA regulations, noting that critics view the 95 percent test participation requirement "as a punitive requirement for States with high numbers of parents choosing to opt their students out of statewide assessments." The department responded that without such a requirement, "there is no guarantee that schools will not encourage certain students to avoid testing all together."[33] If you believe that the standards, tests, and accountability mechanisms are good and fair, then it follows that you do not want people gaming the system and excluding poor test takers. But the Obama administration evinced little sympathy for parents who contest standards-based reform or envision a different kind of education for their children.

In March 2017, the Trump administration released a revised template for state education authorities to submit their ESSA applications. State applications must describe how the state factors the requirement for 95 percent student participation in statewide assessments into their accountability systems.[34] This rule makes only a nominal change from the Obama administration's rules, and many states in 2017 are submitting ESSA plans that penalize schools with a high percentage of students refusing the tests.[35] Tennessee, for example, has said that, "any school not hitting 95 percent participation for all students, or for subgroups of students, would get an F grade on the achievement indicator for the corresponding group of students."[36] Despite the hopes of some conservatives, the Trump administration seems committed to using Title I funds to keep states using the Common Core standards, or a facsimile, and aligned assessments.[37]

A New Accountability Paradigm?

Many people blame opposition to the Common Core on implementation. Perhaps improving the tests and accountability mechanisms will generate more parental support for the standards. This is the wager of Linda Darling-Hammond, Gene Wilhoit, and Linda Pittenger in their 2014 article, "Accountability for College and Career Readiness: Developing a New Paradigm." Unfortunately, the authors maintain that experts—rather than communities, educators, and parents—should still make crucial decisions about education standards.

The essay argues that the framework of No Child Left Behind is sound but must be built upon to achieve the benefits of systemic education reform: "It is clear that the NCLB legacy that 'every child matters' represents an evolution in our thinking. It is also clear that our current strategies are not sufficient to ensure that, indeed, every child will be enabled to learn the higher-order skills that they need to acquire to succeed in today's world."[38] To improve the schools, one must work simultaneously on improving learning, teaching, and assessment.

Regarding learning, the authors support the Common Core standards but think they need to be fully implemented and supplemented. The testing regime covers only part of the Common Core standards, neglecting, for instance, the speaking and listening standards. Schools should also teach socio-emotional skills that enable people to succeed in college and careers, including cognitive strategies, learning skills and techniques, and transition knowledge and skills.[39]

Darling-Hammond, Wilhoit, and Pittenger also contend that schools must have sufficient resources to deliver meaningful learning: "Federal, state, and local education agencies must themselves meet certain standards of delivery while school-based educators and students are expected to meet certain standards of practice and learning. Thus, in addition to learning standards that rely on many kinds of data, accountability must encompass resource standards."[40] This argument sounds like an equity argument insofar as it calls for greater distribution of resources, but it is also an excellence argument in its focus on providing resources that lead to greater educational outputs. Resource allocation ensures "equitable access to high-quality *curriculum* and instructional materials that support students in learning the standards."[41]

Finally, standards-based reform requires proper teacher training and professional development in order to work. Teaching licenses should require educators to have a track record of "supporting diverse learners to meet challenging standards," for example. Schools should require professional development in teaching the standards, and the state should send inspectors to schools to ensure they are following those standards, and so forth. Accountability works only if everyone in the system is held accountable for doing his or her job.[42]

The main thrust of the article, and the one that buttresses its claim to create a new paradigm, is the need to rethink assessment to drive authentic learning. The authors accept the need for the Common Core state tests; their goal is to shift the focus of the school year from "external summative events to formative assessments that can be used in more efficient and effective ways."[43] For example, schools should enable students to make portfolio collections, mathematics applications, and scientific investigations. Local assessments can make students "agents in their own learning" by producing "software solutions, engineering designs, data collection and analysis, literary anthologies, topological maps, artistic productions, and museum exhibits."[44] To maintain oversight, "the state provides common rubrics, training for scoring, and auditing to ensure that these can be scored reliably."[45] The goal is to assess a wider range of information that in turn will incentivize educators to support deeper learning.

The authors think that genuine accountability "must involve communities, along with professional educators and governments, in establishing goals and contributing to their attainment."[46] Local communities must be involved "in decision making about budgets and programs," and school climate surveys can be used to hold schools accountable to students, parents, and adults who work at the school.[47] The authors restrict, however, the claims community members can make on the schools. Genuine accountability "must attend to parents' desires and students' rights to be taught *relevant skills* that will matter for their future success."[48] The authors do not entertain the possibility that communities may have a different conception of skills that they want their schools to teach.

From a democratic perspective, Darling-Hammond, Wilhoit, and Pittenger's proposal gives parents, educators, and citizens little role in creating or choosing the education standards themselves. In their description of an ideal accountability system in a "51st State," they say that the "state pursues *meaningful learning* by . . . establishing college- and career-ready standards anchored in core academic knowledge and skills that recognize competencies considered by higher education, employers, and parents as critical to success."[49] Throughout the essay, the authors assume the permanence, legitimacy, and goodness of the Common Core standards. There is no official procedure to revise the Common Core standards, and the authors evince little interest in pursuing that path even if possible. States and communities can set goals for how to reach the standards, but they may not eschew the Common Core or "college- and career-ready standards."

Furthermore, the essay's primary solution to creating a new paradigm is to increase the federal and state government's reach into more and more aspects of the education system. For instance, the authors call upon teachers to exercise more judgment in selecting and designing assignments and assessments, but they also call for "common rubrics" and "auditing processes" to ensure that teachers are following the standards.[50] Micromanaging teachers will not satisfy parents who think that the standards are part of the problem. The authors do not trust locals to determine the destination of the education voyage. It is telling that their article does not use the concept of democracy.

Democracy and Local Education Control

Why should we care about democracy as a criterion of education? Why is it important to entrust communities to run public schools? And what is the alternative to national education standards? To address these questions, I will reconstruct ideas from one of America's greatest philosophers and educators—John Dewey (1859–1952).

We should care about democracy as a criterion of education, according to Dewey, because it makes the educational experience more rewarding for teachers and students. Teachers teach with more energy when they have a say in the goals, pace, and activities of the classroom. In his essay, "The Classroom Teacher," Dewey explains that "if you are engaged in carrying out plans and ideas of one person, you do not, and cannot, throw yourself into it with the same enthusiasm and wholeheartedness, or same desire to learn and improve, that you do when you are carrying out plans and ideas which you yourselves have had some share in developing."[51] Every person in a classroom is a complex, living being with a unique history, personality, and combination of talents and interests. It stifles the teacher's vitality when they must follow scripted lesson plans. For Dewey, teachers who choose the activities, assign their favorite books, organize field trips, and so forth, tend to put their hearts and minds into it, making a classroom experience more exciting and engaging.

By the same logic, students who take charge of their own education, with appropriate guidance from teachers and mentors, learn more than those who go through the motions in the classroom. Dewey criticizes traditional education for "its passivity of attitude, its mechanical massing of children, its uniformity of curriculum and method." Instead, he calls for a Copernican revolution in education whereby "the child becomes the sun about which the appliances of education revolve."[52] This idea must be immediately qualified because Dewey did not want children left to their own devices. In his view, teachers play a crucial role in introducing children to the best that civilization has to offer on any topic that interests them. The goal is to train musically inclined children, for example, to play classical and contemporary compositions so that they may in turn write their own music. The purpose of education is for students to master the knowledge of the past and present so that they may contribute when it is their turn. "Let the child's nature fulfill its own destiny, revealed to you in whatever of science and art and industry the world now holds as its own."[53]

It is important to entrust communities to run public schools, according to Dewey, because this is a way to experience democracy as a way of life. In his 1903 essay, "Democracy in Education," Dewey explains that democracy entails teachers having "a share in determining the conditions and the aims of [their] own work." Upon the whole, the work of the world is better done "through the free and mutual harmonizing of different individuals" than "when planned, arranged, and directed by a few, no matter how wise or of how good intent that few."[54] For Dewey, democracy is a social arrangement whereby everybody can express their own individuality in ways that enrich the community. Schools can be an enchanting space where everybody acts and is acted upon with dignity. We should be careful about attributing too much influence to Dewey's ideas upon public education in the twentieth century.[55] Still, there was a time after World War II where schools often did provide teachers and students opportunities to develop their own interests and talents in supportive communities.[56]

Furthermore, schools can train children to perform their role as active citizens who can spread democratic norms through the family, the workplace, and the community. It is not the case that students first become educated in literacy and numeracy and then become adults confident in their ability to change the world. There is no sharp distinction between education *for* democracy and democracy *in* education: the more you grow up in a democratic community, the better you will be prepared to serve your adult roles as citizen. Schools need to teach children from a young age that their voice matters in how the community governs itself. Once children exit the formal educational institutions, they will be curious, assertive adults who, if well-socialized, will be interested in working with others to create a society of "equitably distributed interests"—that is, a democracy.[57]

Keeping education power local means that schooling tends to be more vibrant, people feel more connected to their communities, and children learn what democracy means by seeing it in practice every day. For Dewey, democracy in all areas of life promotes "a better quality of human experience, one which is more widely accessible and enjoyed, than do non-democratic and anti-democratic forms of life."[58]

In *Democracy and Education*, Dewey sees the problem with entrusting the nation-state with control of the education system. Though rulers may pay lip service to the social aims of education, they often are "simply interested in such training as will make their subjects better tools for their own intentions."[59] Dewey thinks that the federal government may play a role in providing the essential material resources for a well-rounded education experience: "School facilities must be secured of such amplitude and efficiency as will in fact and not simply in name discount the effects of economic inequalities, and secure to all wards of the nation equality of equipment for their future careers."[60] The original legislative heading of ESEA Title I was "Financial Assistance to Local Educational Agencies for the Education of Children of Low-Income Families." From a Deweyan perspective, this name conveys a proper role of the federal government in supporting without manipulating public education.

The alternative to national education standards, for Dewey, is to empower parents, educators, children, and community members to decide together how to teach literature, math, science, history, and other fields of inquiry. "Democracy must begin at home, and its home is the neighborly community."[61] From a democratic perspective, it is more important that communities control the schools than that every school use any particular pedagogy. A democratic educational landscape is a garden with many flowers.

Local Education Control—for Everyone

A proponent of national education standards may reply: surely the country can agree on a minimum set of education standards to ensure that all children graduate from high school ready for college and careers. The problem that we have seen in this book, however, is that every definition of "minimal" education standards is controversial. Reasonable people disagree over how to teach literacy, numeracy, science, history, and sexual health. In our country, we are witnessing powerful people granting themselves the right to decide how nearly all American children are educated. And many parents, teachers, and educators, including those in historically disadvantaged communities, are saying no to top-down, standards-based reform. People want a say in what and how the local schools teach children.[62]

Consider, for example, the battle over local education control in Oakland, California. In *A Different View of Urban Schools: Civil Rights, Critical Race Theory, and Unexplored Realities*, Kitty Kelly Epstein shows that white, business-oriented school boards did wrong by many Oakland students between the 1920s and the early 1960s. However, in the late 1960s, the civil rights movement brought a wave of non-white school boards to power. These school boards "initiated important new policies that have helped to move the country forward in educational equity. Oakland's movement won victories in minority hiring and contracting, stopped a state takeover, and rejected racially insensitive textbooks."[63] White political and economic elites argued that the Oakland school board was corrupt, nepotistic, and concerned with black jobs rather than black students. For Epstein, however, these charges were wrong, mean-spirited, and concealed how political and economic elites wanted to control Oakland's school budgets and curricula. For Epstein, "to remove the power of school boards is to further disenfranchise African Americans as a group."[64] Turning the tables on those who say that top-down education reform is justified because of equity concerns, Epstein replies, "School governance is a messy but critical aspect of civil rights."[65]

Or consider the situation at Dyett High School in Chicago. In 2015, Mayor Rahm Emanuel said his administration would close the school and reopen it as an arts high school, but community activists wanted it to have a focus on green technology. Twelve community members went on a hunger strike to oppose the mayor's plans and advocate local control. Brother Jitu, one of the strikers, said, "I'm on this hunger strike because we were rendered voiceless. We met with every bureaucrat, attended every sham hearing and smiled when we should have roared. We have a right to a significant voice in the education of the children we are raising, in the decisions about how our tax dollars are spent. Bronzeville has spoken. Time for the decision-makers to listen."[66] People in Chicago, Philadelphia, Detroit, and Baltimore want to make crucial decisions about their children's education.[67]

One way that parents and students of color signal their disapproval of standards-based reform is to refuse to take Common Core high-stakes tests. According to Jesse Hagopian in a 2016 article for *The Progressive*, "while it's true that currently the students opting out are disproportionately white, to portray opting out as a white people thing is to make invisible the important leadership role that people of color have played around the country. Chicago Teachers Union president Karen Lewis, a black woman, is one of the most important leaders in the country against corporate education reform, and she led the union in the 'Let Us Teach!' campaign against high-stakes testing. The Black opt out rate reached 10 percent in Chicago last year." He continues, "One of the largest student protests against high-stakes testing in U.S. history occurred last spring when many hundreds of students in New Mexico—at schools that served 90% Latino students—walked out of school and refused to take the new Common Core exams. In Ohio, a recent study shows that communities of color and low-income communities opt out at nearly the same rates as whiter and wealthier ones."[68]

Local education control is not a silver bullet to solve America's education woes. There is no guarantee that enlightened pedagogues will be in charge anywhere; the choice is whether we want to put all of our eggs in one national basket or let thousands of smaller-scale conflicts about curricula rage across the country. Political scientists have shown that we live in an era of economic-elite domination where the affluent have substantially more influence over federal government policies than ordinary citizens. If there is one wheel of American education policy, then oligarchs are likely to grab it.[69] In this context, democrats should advocate local education control. Local schools will often need improvement, but parents, educators, and others should work within their communities to make a positive change.

There are many good ways to educate children. A democracy should have space for schools run on the educational philosophies of David Coleman, John Dewey, E. D. Hirsch Jr., Ignatius of Loyola, James Milgram, Maria Montessori, Sandra Stotsky, Rudolph Steiner, Jason Zimba, and people we do not even know about yet. A democracy should make room for International Baccalaureate programs, French immersion schools, engineering courses, theater programs, and independent study projects. Reasonable people have different ideas about how to educate children. Rather than stifle dissent, let us encourage people to help run local schools on a variety of different models. Our schools, and our politics, will be better when many people have a meaningful voice in how children are educated.

Democracy and the Test Refusal Movement

....

The fuel for writing this book is my love for my children. When I think about my children's education, I think about my own. Sure, I had to do busywork and take tests as a student. But most of those memories have faded away. What remains are the enchanting things I did as a student: editing a newspaper in second grade; performing in the fourth-grade play; making journals about the presidential election in sixth grade; doing algebraic proofs in seventh grade; competing on the debate team in high school; and writing research papers where I chose the topic. The Common Core does not necessarily mean the instant and total termination of all of those kinds of activities. But the Common Core does have real-world effects, some of them good and some of them bad, and honesty compels us to acknowledge that it prunes the curriculum.[1] What gets tested gets taught, and schools across the country are removing things that do not fit in the new education regime.[2]

I want my children to have a well-rounded education that encourages habits of lifelong learning. Schools ought to impart teachers' knowledge and passion to children who have their own interests and talents. Children should do meaningful projects that engage their minds, hearts, and hands. Kids ought to tend gardens, build structures, and go on field trips, not spend their days on computers. Like many parents today, I oppose the Common Core because I see every day that it leads to an inferior education based on taking or preparing for standardized tests. The fact that many powerful

FIGURE E.1 "More Teaching, Less Testing."
Source: Courtesy of New York State Allies for Public Education

people send their own children to private schools with a different kind of education confirms our suspicion that the Common Core is canned food for the masses. That is unacceptable for many parents. We will keep fighting until our kids get fresh food (figure E.1).[3]

One way that parents can signal their disapproval of the current education regime is to refuse the tests. Reformers often view high-stakes testing as the lever to force teachers to teach and students to learn standards. The Race to the Top program, for instance, incentivized states to adopt common standards, implement common assessments, and improve teacher and principal effectiveness based on performance.[4] In other words, the Obama administration incentivized states to adopt the Common Core, administer aligned tests such as the PARCC and SBAC, and fire teachers and principals in schools that do not demonstrate sufficient test score growth, in order to receive a Race to the Top grant or a No Child Left Behind waiver. The Every Student Succeeds Act maintains the federal requirement that states administer high-stakes tests of "challenging" academic standards which, for all intents and purposes, means the Common Core.[5] High-stakes testing locks national education standards into place.

Parents had little say in how the Common Core was created or adopted, but we do have a choice about whether our kids take the tests. In the spring of 2015, more than two hundred thousand New York students in grades 3–8 opted out of the end-of-year Common Core tests, and that number increased in subsequent years despite a coordinated effort by the state education department to quell the movement.[6] A remarkable feature of the Common Core test refusal movement is its diversity. Parents of different ethnic and racial backgrounds, in the city, suburbs, and rural areas, with different political ideologies and educational preferences, have coalesced into the test refusal movement. A silver lining of the Common Core initiative for me is that I have made friends with people around the state, country, and world whom I otherwise probably would never have met.[7]

In this epilogue, I present three accounts of leaders of the test refusal movement. One is by Michael V. McGill, a Scarsdale superintendent who helped launch the test refusal movement in 2001; the second is by Michael Hynes and Lori Koerner, a superintendent and elementary school principal, respectively, on Long Island; and the third is by Jamaal Bowman, a principal of a Title I school in the Bronx. At the end, I explain how this book attempts to give focus to the test refusal movement. The problem is not just the testing, or the accountability mechanisms, or even the Common Core: the problem is the idea of national education standards in our current political environment. Democracy means entrusting communities to take charge of the schools, including in the all-important matter of academic standards that express a philosophy of education.

Test Refusal in Scarsdale

Scarsdale is a wealthy suburb of New York City. In 2001, parents of one hundred eighth graders, a third of the class, pledged to keep their children at home on the day of the end-of-year test. This revolt against the New York State Education Department preceded the No Child Left Behind Act, but it presaged the contemporary test refusal movement, particularly in New York. In *Race to the Bottom*, Michael

McGill explains why he tolerated, or rather encouraged, parents to resist the state's testing mandates.

Born into a family of educators, McGill had a forty-year career in school leadership, including serving as superintendent of the Scarsdale school district from 1998 to 2014. According to McGill, good educators need curiosity, interest, and enthusiasm. "Teachers cultivate these qualities through minute-by-minute interactions, making thoughtful judgments about the next step each student must take to realize her or his promise. The coursing heart of a real education is not a forced march in pursuit of higher scores, but the personal encounter between teacher and student. It depends on adults who are able to negotiate delicate webs of human interaction."[8]

Standards, however, do not change for the unique individuals in the classroom or community. Standards say what is important for students to learn, and the flip side of rigor is that schools lose flexibility to deviate from the norm. "Test-centric curriculums and budget slashing have caused many school districts to curtail or eliminate 'nonessentials' like art, music, physical education, and world languages. Far too many educators feel disempowered and demoralized."[9]

Fortunately, McGill was in a position to do something. The school board hired him knowing that he opposed standards-based reform, and he had the support of his community. Scarsdale students regularly did well on standardized tests and earned admission into prestigious colleges and universities. Scarsdale was not refusing the tests because it was scared of the results; it was refusing because the community wanted a better kind of education for its kids. At the time, McGill wrote a letter to parents saying, "Excesses of the standards movement have promoted lock-step education. They've diverted attention from important local goals, highlighted simplistic and sometimes inappropriate tests, needlessly promoted similarity in curriculum and teaching. To the extent they've caused education to regress to a state average, they've undermined excellence."[10]

The *New York Times*, the *Washington Post*, National Public Radio, CNN, and other news outlets covered the story of Scarsdale's revolt. A Regent, one of the people entrusted with making education policy in the state, contacted the Scarsdale board of education and said that the district should disavow the boycott and force students to take the tests. The Commissioner of Education called Scarsdale's actions "a serious case of cheating." The state education department insinuated that the state could take over the school district if it was not complying with state law, regulation, and directives. Eventually, McGill and the Scarsdale school board stopped its protest.[11]

In *Race to the Bottom*, published over a decade after the revolt, McGill still sounds hurt about the response: "In the midst of a corporate-style crusade to transform public education, the worries in an affluent community didn't elicit much sympathy. There was some public interest in the mothers who'd organized the boycott, as well as some mockery of 'soccer moms.' At the very best, the public and the press seemed ambivalent about the story."[12] To its critics, Scarsdale's actions looked like a defense of privilege rather than of the principles of progressive education and local control.

Nonetheless, McGill defends the test refusal movement as a noble effort. He shares a letter from a New York City teacher who writes, "It's refreshing to see a place with common sense and an obvious respect for teachers, students, and the entire school community. Thanks for helping us fight the good fight."[13]

According to a 2016 Teachers College Columbia University report on the opt-out movement, "the typical opt out activist is a highly educated, white, married, politically liberal parent." The test refusal movement is 46 percent Democratic, 15 percent Republican, and 33 percent independent, and based primarily in wealthier suburbs, including, in New York, Westchester County and Long Island.[14] Though the movement is diverse, it also leans liberal, white, and wealthy, which is why some test defenders started a Twitter hash tag: #optoutsowhite.

The test refusal movement, however, does not speak just for the Scarsdales of the country. In the next two sections, we consider how other test refusal leaders contend that working-class or historically disadvantaged communities should also refuse the tests.

Test Refusal in Patchogue-Medford

Patchogue-Medford School District is one of the largest on Long Island and the epicenter of the contemporary test refusal movement. In Pat-Med (as it's called), 52 percent of the students are on the free and reduced lunch program, 38 percent of the student body is Hispanic, and several schools are in the Title I program. It is a blue-collar school district with many children whose parents are firefighters, police officers, and teachers. In 2017, 76 percent of the students in the district refused to take the end-of-year Common Core tests, including 90 percent of the students at Tremont Elementary. The superintendent of Pat-Med, Michael Hynes, EdD, trained at New York University, Stony Brook University, and Harvard University, and is a reader of child psychologists such as Jean Piaget, Abraham Maslow, and Lawrence Kohlberg. The principal at Tremont is Lori Koerner, a teacher for twenty years and now an administrator and advocate for whole child education. With the support of their school board, they have become a thorn in the side of the state education department that wants at least 95 percent of students at all schools to take the test. Stated positively: they have become spokespeople for parents who sense that school could be a happier and more holistic environment than it is now in the Common Core era.

Hynes and Koerner have been vocal critics of the Common Core standards and high-stakes testing. In an *Education Week* blog, for instance, Hynes lambastes the US Department of Education and the New York State Education Department for advocating the standards and aligned tests: "I don't recall hearing anything about testimonies from experts when the Common Core Standards or tests were developed. I think Bill Gates, the Koch brothers and Pearson were contacted however. This is one of the biggest travesties. Big business prevailed." For Hynes, the New York Regents Reform agenda is a local manifestation of what the Finnish scholar Pasi Sahlberg calls the Global Education Reform Movement (GERM). Democracy, professional responsibility, and plain decency demand that people push back against standards-based reform that, in practice, can mean testing children to the point of tears and self-abuse.[15]

The motivation for the test refusal movement, however, is primarily positive rather than negative. When one talks with Hynes and Koerner, or tours the Pat-Med school district, or reads the district's literature, one is struck by all the things they want to do.[16] They talk about the "PEAS" formula: Physical Growth+Emotional Growth+Academic Growth+Social Growth=Human Potential. The "Road to Success" plan for years 2016–2021 includes such things as professional development regarding play, project-based learning, and the benefits of recess; interdisciplinary teaching and learning; courses on and opportunities for all students to meditate and learn yoga; an increase in co-curricular activities; more student time with guidance counselors; and the addition of a dissertation for seniors.[17] Hynes garnered state and national attention for doubling the amount of time that Pat-Med elementary students get for recess each day, and Pat-Med is looking for ways to incorporate more unstructured play into the curriculum. The district's philosophy is that sometimes less is more.

It is a sign of the times that the state education department views Pat-Med as a threat rather than a laboratory of promising ideas. Hynes and Koerner favor differentiating instruction, especially for elementary students, and they speak of cultivating the interests, talents, and potential of each child. National education standards promise to set the exact same bar for all students—regardless of their strengths or weaknesses in any particular academic area or their life circumstances—and the claim of rigor is another way of saying "inflexible." Hynes and Koerner believe in pushing children to develop their abilities—that is, they favor one conception of high standards—but they think that standards-based reform is educating children right out of their joy and creativity. According to Hynes,

"We are using the wrong drivers to change education and we are going at light speed down a road of possibly ensuring that students only know how to bubble in test sheets, become proficient test takers and graduate into standardized widgets."[18]

The Pat-Med team does not want to dictate to the rest of the country how to educate children. They would be happy if more schools offered yoga and meditation, but their main political point is that communities, educators, parents, and children should make meaningful decisions about the local schools' philosophy of education. Test refusal is a way to let distant bureaucrats and political and economic elites know that communities want to set their own education aims.

Test Refusal in the Bronx

In 2016, at Cornerstone Academy for Social Action (CASA), an acclaimed middle school in the Bronx, one-fourth of its student body opted out of Common Core tests.[19] Jamaal Bowman is the founder and principal of CASA. He studied sports management at the University of New Haven before deciding to become an educator. Then, during New York Mayor Michael Bloomberg's administration, Bowman submitted a small-school application to open a middle school. Influenced by scholars such as Howard Gardner, Tony Wagner, and Ken Robinson, but also by rap artists such as Boogie Down Productions and Public Enemy, whose images grace his office's walls, Bowman has become a leader of the test refusal movement.[20] He explains his thinking in a blog called "The Tyranny of Standardized Testing" that has garnered national attention and notoriety.[21]

Bowman describes the reality of high-stakes testing in Title I schools. Every year, teachers, parents, and children live in fear of whether the end-of-year test scores will be high enough to avoid the students being held back or the principal and much of his or her staff being fired. In five years as an elementary school teacher at the start of his career, Bowman had four different principals. Poor and immigrant families have to survive the chaos that such turnover causes in the schools.

Policymakers advocate turning poor-testing public schools into privately managed charter schools, with their record of higher test scores. Bowman responds that charter schools achieve higher test scores because they expel poor-scoring students and focus almost exclusively on test preparation. He sympathizes with the charter school student who says that it feels like prison: "Oppressive assessments, lead to oppressive schools, and oppressed students." Bowman is a positive person who loves to teach and loves his community, but he sees that standards-based reform means that many minority and poor children get little exposure to art, music, theater, science, or history.

Bowman has heard the argument that schools should concentrate on teaching poor and minority children the basic literacy and numeracy skills that they will likely need once they enter the job market. Schools should teach these skills, he responds, but they also need to provide all children with culture, varied learning experiences, and a holistic education. Bowman looks to progressive public and private schools and thinks that the same philosophy of education should apply in the inner city. All children deserve to go to a school that celebrates the unique qualities of each teacher and student. According to Bowman,

> Whenever government becomes destructive of its people, it's time for the people to alter or abolish the government. When parents choose to opt out of the state tests, they are using civil disobedience to alter the government for its destructive high stakes standardized testing practices. Parents are opting out because the current implementation of standardized testing perpetuates a mental model of oppression for parents, teachers, and students. Parents are opting out because they love their children and they love America. Parents want to create a future rooted in America's ideals that's brighter for their children

and grandchildren. A future, not rooted in the poverty, war, pain and suffering of today. But a future rooted in love and happiness.

Bowman celebrates the test refusal movement for uniting people of all races and backgrounds to combat injustice. The movement is not about Democrat or Republican, black or white, rich or poor: it is about parents working with other parents to stop harmful educational practices.

Bowman's essay attained notoriety for its theme that high-stakes testing "is a form of modern day slavery."[22] If high-stakes testing oppresses kids' spirits and helps build a school-to-prison pipeline, then the comparison may be apt.

Parents and educators are howling in pain that the shoe of standardized testing does not fit.[23] As a participant in the test refusal movement, I have seen many parents cry about what school is doing to their children. I have witnessed parents share their concerns on social media and at community meetings, and I have also observed think-tank policy experts and school administrators ridicule parents and dismiss their concerns. The test refusal movement is a way for people affected to say that the Common Core experiment is failing teachers, students, communities, and our democracy.

Giving Focus to the Test Refusal Movement

According to a report on the 2015 opt-out movement in New Jersey, people refused the tests because of skepticism about high-stakes testing, fury over Common Core implementation, teacher union opposition to accountability, and confusion about graduation requirements. The authors do not even countenance the possibility that people have a legitimate grievance against the standards themselves.[24] In this book, I have aimed to give focus to the test refusal movement and argue that democracies should not pursue the project of national education standards.

The Common Core standards are, in the words of New York High School Principal of the Year Carol Burris, a "lemon."[25] In this book, I have described the problems with Common Core close reading and its prohibitions on students sharing their own thoughts and feelings. The Common Core does not prepare children to exercise personal or political autonomy; it teaches children to follow orders. Common Core math progressions do not enable most students to take calculus in time to pursue a STEM major in college. The Common Core prepares most children for community college or vocational programs, not the kinds of careers that many parents dream of for their own children. The Next Generation Science Standards and the College Board Advanced Placement curriculum frameworks share many of the same features, and problems, as the Common Core, particularly the focus on skills that can be tested on computers.

If we say that most Americans agree that Common Core 1.0 has failed, should we try a Common Core 2.0?[26] This book has presented arguments why another experiment with national education standards would likely lead to similar problems. National education standards, in the current landscape, virtually always lead to performance expectations that can be assessed online. National education standards empower one faction to impose their education vision on the country. They alienate citizens from the local schools and civic life in general. They do not accommodate students who possess different skill sets that can lead to inventions and breakthroughs. And national education standards narrow the curriculum, particularly in low-income communities that they are ostensibly supposed to help.

Many parents wish that they had a meaningful voice in the local schools. Right now, state education departments have entrusted local education authorities to implement, but not change or criticize, standards-based education reform. In the present era, school boards around the country can hire or fire superintendents, but they cannot choose an alternative to the Common Core. In this book, I have argued that our country should make a course correction and grant substantive educational power to communities. Some communities may make choices that we would not make, but that is what it means to live in a free society. The federal and state government may supplement school budgets, but they should respect the wishes of the community to run the schools.

Pedagogically, schools do a better job when they have the enthusiastic support of parents and people in the neighborhood. Politically, locally controlled schools teach children and adults the skills and dispositions to make democracy a way of life.

Notes

··

Introduction: Do We Need a Common Core?

1. Timothy Shanahan, an author of *Treasures*, served on the development team of the Common Core ELA standards. McGraw-Hill has discontinued *Treasures* and replaced it with *Wonders*.

2. Tampio, "Do We Need a Common Core?"

3. Ravitch, "Why I Cannot Support."

4. Ravitch, *National Standards*.

5. Layton, "How Bill Gates."

6. Ravitch, "Why I Cannot Support."

7. Cited in Ravitch, "Fatal Flaw."

8. Ibid. See also Cody, "The Secret Sixty."

9. Miller and Carlsson-Paige, "A Tough Critique."

10. Ravitch, "Fatal Flaw."

11. Ravitch, "Why I Cannot Support."

12. Ibid.

13. Decker, "Algebra Pass Rates."

14. See Ravitch, *Death and Life*, prologue.

15. Henderson, Peterson, and West, "The 2015 EdNext Poll."

16. Klein, "ESEA Reauthorization."

17. Rhodes, "Learning Citizenship?"

18. On how the education reform movement has sought to displace educational liberalism (or progressivism), see Rhodes, *An Education in Politics*; Mehta, *The Allure of Order*.

19. See Tampio, "In Praise of Dewey."

20. On how the human capital argument is transforming education policy around the world, see Spring, *Economization of Education.*

21. Duncan, "Thinking beyond Silver Bullets."

22. See Howell, "Obama's Race to the Top."

23. Duncan, "Thinking beyond Silver Bullets."

24. Hernández, "New Education Secretary."

25. For an amusing account of how the Charles M. Schulz Museum in California offers programs that align with the Common Core, see Braun, "Good Grief!"

26. Duncan, "Duncan Pushes Back."

Chapter One: Arguments for National Education Standards

1. *American Educator*, cover.

2. On the legacy of this article, see Vinovskis, "Systemic Educational Reform." For a recent iteration of its thesis, see Harris et al., *A Principled Federal Role.*

3. Smith and O'Day, "Systemic School Reform," 238.

4. Mehta, "How Paradigms Create Politics."

5. Smith and O'Day, "Systemic School Reform," 238.

6. Ibid., 237.

7. Ibid., 246.

8. See also Smith, O'Day, and Cohen, "National Curriculum, American Style," 10–17, 40–47.

9. Smith and O'Day, "Systemic School Reform," 247–248.

10. Ibid., 254.

11. Ibid., 261.

12. Mehta, *The Allure of Order*, 207–208.

13. Darling-Hammond, *Flat World*, 28.

14. Ibid., 51.

15. Ibid., 52.

16. Ibid., 54.

17. See Darling-Hammond, Williamson, and Hyler, "Securing the Right to Learn," 281–296.

18. Ravitch, "Linda Darling-Hammond."

19. Darling-Hammond, *Flat World*, 328.

20. Rhodes, "Progressive Policy Making."

21. *Lasting Impact*, 4. See also Hanushek, Peterson, and Woessmann, *Endangering Prosperity*.

22. *Lasting Impact*, 2.

23. Ibid., 8.

24. Ibid., 13–14.

25. Elkind, "Business Gets Schooled," 48–60.

26. I thank Brenda Wellburn for telling me this point.

27. Bindewald, Tannebaum, and Womac, "Common Core and Democratic Education," 4.

28. Ibid., 1.

29. Ibid.

30. Ibid., 7.

31. Ibid., 9.

32. See also Levinson, "Democracy, Accountability, and Education," 125–144.

Chapter Two: Arguments against National Education Standards

1. Meyer, "Civil Society and Education," 13–34.

2. Hamilton, Madison, and Jay, *The Federalist Papers*, 48.

3. "Liberty is to faction what air is to fire, an aliment without which it instantly expires. But it could not be less folly to abolish liberty, which is essential to political life, because it nourishes faction, than it would be to wish the annihilation of air, which is essential to animal life, because it imparts to fire its destructive agency." Ibid.

4. Ibid., 52.

5. Ibid.

6. Ibid., 264.

7. See Rhodes, *An Education in Politics*, 18–19.

8. On the groups and individuals that coordinated the Common Core State Standards Initiative, see Schneider, *Common Core Dilemma*.

9. Tocqueville, *Democracy in America*, xvii.

10. Ibid., 482.

11. Ibid., 489.

12. Ibid., 486, 487, 488.

13. Rhodes, "Learning Citizenship," 183.

14. See Levinson, "Democracy, Accountability, and Education."

15. Rhodes, "Learning Citizenship," 183.

16. On how John Dewey provides democratic grounds to oppose national education standards, see Tampio, "Democracy and National Education Standards."

17. Zhao, *World Class Learners*, 123.

18. Duncan, "Arne Duncan's Remarks."

19. Zhao, *World Class Learners*, 127.

20. See also Tienken, *Defying Standardization*, particularly chapter 3.

21. Zhao, *World Class Learners*, 137.

22. Ibid., 135.

23. Ibid., 133.

24. See Meier, *Will Standards Save*.

25. Rhodes, "Progressive Policy Making," 519–544.

26. "The rhetoric of the education reform movement champions CCS as a tool to create civil rights opportunities for Black and Latin students, but the reality is that the new CCS-aligned assessments are used to unfairly label students, punish teachers, and close schools." "Arguments," 3.

27. Vasquez Heilig, Cole, and Aguilar, "From Dewey," 137.

28. Ibid., 142.

29. Standards are conceptually distinct from testing and accountability mechanisms, but at least since Smith and O'Day's 1990 article, "Systemic School Reform," education reform policies such as Race to the Top bundle them together.

30. Heilig, et al., "From Dewey," 136. See also Hamilton, et al., *Standards-Based Accountability*, 102–107.

31. Heilig, et al., "From Dewey," 143.

32. Williams, "Rhythm and Bruise."

33. One response to this situation is to write arts education standards and lobby to have them included in the curriculum. On how this strategy can backfire, strategically and in regards to the quality of arts education, see Heilig, et al., "From Dewey," 138.

Chapter Three: English Standards, Close Reading, and Testing

1. All references to the Common Core ELA standards may be found at "Common Core State Standards English Language Arts."

2. Steiner and Coleman, *Bringing the Common Core*, 2.

3. Reckhow, *Follow the Money*; Layton, "How Bill Gates"; Strauss, "New Book."

4. On Susan Pimentel's role in writing the Common Core ELA standards, see Schneider, *Common Core Dilemma*, 108–114.

5. Coleman, "Cultivating Wonder."

6. Goldstein, "The Schoolmaster."

7. Ibid., 3.

8. Ibid., 4.

9. Ibid., 11.

10. The final anchor standard demands that students "read and comprehend complex literary and informational texts independently and proficiently."

11. Coleman, "Cultivating Wonder," 19–20.

12. Ibid., 20.

13. Ibid., 22.

14. Heitin, "Free Teaching Website."

15. See Kane, Kerr, and Pianta, *Designing Teacher Evaluation Systems*.

16. "Every Student Succeeds Act."

17. Felton, "How the Common Core."

18. College Board, "Annual Results."

19. Dudley, "College Board."

20. Robinson, Katzman, and Staff of the Princeton Review, *Cracking the New Sat*, 21.

21. Ibid., 22.

22. Ibid., 25.

23. Ibid., 34.

24. Ibid., 76.

25. Cited in Casey, "The Gettysburg Address," 60.

26. Robinson, et al., *Cracking the New SAT*, 433.

27. On how the two main Common Core testing consortia (PARCC, SBAC) use computers to grade written essays, see Haimson, "Should You Trust." See also Winterhalter, "Computer Grading."

28. Dewey, *Democracy and Education*, 76.

29. Ibid., 77.

30. See Stern, "New York's School Reform."

31. Dewey, *Democracy and Education*, 200.

32. Cowles, "Child's Play."

33. Ravitch, "What's Not to Like."

34. Dewey, *The School and Society*, 8.

35. Ibid., 19.

36. Dewey, *Democracy and Education*, 108.

37. Ibid., 112.

38. Ibid., 90.

39. Katz, "Dear Common Core."

40. Beach, Thein, and Webb, *Teaching to Exceed*, 4.

41. Ibid., 9.

42. Ibid., 23.

43. Cited at ibid., 39.

44. Dewey, *The School and Society*, 37.

45. Steiner and Coleman, *Bringing the Common Core*, 10.

46. On how Dewey influenced public education in the twentieth century, see Tampio, "In Praise of Dewey."

47. Gilens and Page, "Testing Theories."

48. Meier, *Will Standards*, 5.

49. See Epstein, *A Different View*, chapter 4.

Chapter Four: Math Standards, Understanding, and College and Career Readiness

1. Zimba, "Development."

2. Ibid., 5.

3. Ibid., 6.

4. Ibid., 6–7.

5. Ibid., 7.

6. "Common Core State Standards."

7. Danielson, *Common Core Math*.

8. Ibid.

9. Ash, "Common Core Needs Tailoring."

10. "Common Core State Standards," Appendix A.

11. New York State Education Department, "Race to the Top Application," 352; Heitin, "Free Teaching Website."

12. Great Minds, "EngageNY Math Is Eureka Math." See also Politikoff, "How Well Aligned."

13. Heitin, "Approach to Fractions"; Wu, "Phoenix Rising."

14. College Board, "Reach Higher," 2.

15. Gewertz, "Incoming College Board Head."

16. Robinson, et al., *Cracking the New SAT*, 146.

17. Felton, "How the Common Core."

18. Robinson, et al., *Cracking the New SAT*, 158.

19. Ibid., 198.

20. College Board, "SAT Practice Test #6," Question 14.

21. Robinson et al., *Cracking the New SAT*, 180.

22. Beals and Garelick, "Explaining Your Math."

23. Zimba, "When the Standard Algorithm."

24. Milgram, "Review of Final Draft."

25. Milgram and Stotsky, *Can This Country Survive*, 7.

26. Ibid., 9.

27. *What Does It Really Mean.*

28. Milgram and Stotsky, *Can This Country Survive*, 9.

29. Zimba, "Critics' Math Doesn't Add Up."

30. Stern, "The New Math."

31. Burris, "View."

32. Battista, "Research"; Schoenfeld, "The Math Wars."

33. Simon, "Bill Gates."

34. Comment on Bauerlein, "A Concluded Battle."

35. "Snapshot: Tracking the Common Core."

36. Zimba, "Development." See also Weiss, "Innovation Mismatch."

37. Hayes, "How A War Hero."

38. Editorial Board, "Robert Small."

39. Garland, "The Man Behind."

40. Rhodes, "Learning Citizenship?"

41. See Garland, "In Texas."

42. Layton, "How Bill Gates."

*Chapter Five: Science Standards, Scientific Unity,
and the Problem of Sustainability*

1. "Some states have been quiet about their adoption decisions, likely to avoid drumming up the kind of controversy that's characterized the Common Core State Standards." Heitin, "Updated Map."

2. National Research Council, *Framework*, 1, 7.

3. Pruitt, "Next Generation," 145–156.

4. *Next Generation Science Standards.*

5. "Lead State Partners." New York–specific performance expectation codes are highlighted in yellow. The NGSS does not include prekindergarten standards.

6. "NGSS: Executive Summary."

7. "NGSS: Appendix A," 5.

8. See Achieve, "How to Read."

9. "NGSS: Executive Summary."

10. Ibid.

11. Ibid.

12. National Research Council, *Framework*, 52–53.

13. Ibid., 74–75.

14. "Conceptual Shifts."

15. National Research Council, *Framework*, 241.

16. Ibid., 245.

17. Ibid., 30.

18. Ibid., 255.

19. Ibid., 263.

20. Ibid., 262–263.

21. Heiten, "Next Generation Science Tests."

22. "Next Generation Task Portal."

23. See also National Research Council, *Developing Assessments*; Heitin, "Here's What We Know."

24. OECD PISA, *PISA 2015*.

25. Ibid., 4–5.

26. Wysession, "Preparing," 1167.

27. "In the NGSS, rote memorization of the names of clouds or minerals is expressly not to be assessed." Ibid., 1170.

28. Gross, *Final Evaluation*.

29. Ault, *Challenging Science Standards*.

30. Ibid., xvi.

31. Ibid., 7.

32. Ibid., xv.

33. Ibid., xxi.

34. Ibid., xxi.

35. Ibid.

36. "The articulation of 'assessment boundaries' in connection with many standards threatened to place an unwarranted ceiling on important

learning. Yes, teachers can go above and beyond what the boundary suggests, but with time and resources scarce, how many will actually teach students—even advanced students—content and skills that they know in advance 'won't be on the test'?" Gross, *Final Evaluation*, 7.

37. National Research Council, *Framework*, 9.

38. Taylor and Pullmann, "Heartland Institute Experts."

39. See Robelen, "Common Science Standards."

40. Feinstein and Kirchgasler, "Sustainability in Science Education?," 123.

41. Ibid., 128–129.

42. Ibid., 130–131.

43. Ibid., 132–134.

44. Ibid., 121.

45. Ibid., 137.

46. NGSS: For States, By States.

47. Wysession, "Preparing," 1170.

48. National Research Council, *Framework*, 62.

49. Dewey, "The Child and the Curriculum," 286. Dewey's two other critiques of standardization also seem to apply to the NGSS. "When material is directly supplied in the form of a lesson to be learned as a lesson, the connecting links of need and aim are conspicuous for their absence." And "even the most scientific matter, arranged in the most logical fashion, loses this quality, when presented in external ready-made fashion, by the time it gets to the child" (287–288). In other words, NGSS computer simulations may not interest many children, and providing scientific information does not necessarily mean that children will learn to think like scientists.

50. OECD PISA, "Sustainable Fish Farming."

51. Putnam Northern Westchester BOCES, *SCIENCE21*.

52. National Research Council, *Framework*, 262.

53. The New York State Science Education Consortium published a paper in 2013 supporting the state's adoption of the NGSS with reservations. "While the amount of disciplinary content in the NGSS is generally appropriate to meet *minimum* science literacy expectations for *all students*, there are some fundamental concepts and principles missing," and the NGSS is "not sufficient for preparing students who intend to pursue professional careers in science, engineering, and/or technology."

New York State Science Education Consortium, "Position Paper" (italics in original).

54. Gross, *Final Evaluation*, 14.

55. Rogers, "Democracy, Elites and Power."

Chapter Six: History Standards, American Identity, and the Politics of Storytelling

1. Schneider, "Tug of War," 813–831.

2. Ibid., 815.

3. Ibid., 820–821.

4. US Department of Education, "More than $28 Million."

5. Schneider, "Tug of War," 822.

6. Ibid., 828.

7. Lewin, "Backer of Common Core."

8. Hart, et al., *Common Core*.

9. Yi, "College Board."

10. Strauss, "College Board."

11. On how the Next Generation Science Standards (NGSS) and the Advanced Placement (AP) program rely upon the schema of the College Board's *Standards for College Success* (2009), see "Next Generation Science Standards: Appendix C," 3–4.

12. Ibid.

13. Ibid.

14. "Common Core State Standards English Language Arts."

15. National Council for the Social Studies, *College, Career*, 20.

16. Ibid., 56.

17. National Association of Scholars, "Letter Opposing."

18. On the differences between the 2010 and 2014 APUSH curriculum frameworks, see Curry, Sabina, and Loffi, "Advanced Placement," 30–52.

19. National Association of Scholars.

20. Wood, "APUSH," 229–230.

21. Ibid., 229.

22. College Board, "AP Course and Exam Description," 4.

23. Staff of the Princeton Review, *Cracking the AP*, 102.

24. Ibid., 85.

25. Ibid., 51.

26. Ibid., 72.

27. Ibid., 150.

28. Ibid., 104.

29. College Board, *Rubrics*, 6.

30. Ibid., 102.

31. Williams, "JW Proposal."

32. Garcia, "Jeffco Cancels Classes."

33. Bartels, "Jefferson County."

34. College Board, "Statement."

35. Superville, "In Colorado."

36. College Board, "AP Course and Exam Description," 5.

37. Ibid.

38. Hess and Eden, "Surprise."

39. Curry, et al., "Advanced Placement," 36.

40. Eden, *The Mend of History.*

41. Kurtz, "APUSH Revisions."

42. Ibid.

43. Arendt, *The Human Condition*, 192.

44. Arendt, "Reflections on Little Rock," 45–56.

45. See Rhodes, "Learning Citizenship?," 181–220.

46. College Board, "AP Course and Exam Description," 60.

47. Ibid., 58.

48. College Board, "AP United States History 2016 Free-Response Questions."

49. Dewey, "The Principle of Nationality," 288.

Chapter Seven: Sexuality Standards, Gender Identity, and Religious Minorities

1. "National Sexuality Education Standards," 6.

2. Shah, "National Sexuality Standards."

3. Hauser, et al., "Education and the Path."

4. Barr, et al., "Improving Sexuality Education," 396–415.

5. "National Sexuality Education Standards," 5.

6. Shah, "National Sexuality Standards."

7. "National Sexuality Education Standards," 8.

8. Ibid., 7.

9. Hauser, et al., "Education and the Path."

10. "National Sexuality Education Standards," 9.

11. Ibid., 26.

12. Ibid., 27–28.

13. Zimmerman, *Too Hot to Handle*, 87.

14. Fisher, et al., "Perceptions," 7.

15. Steadman, et al., "Parental Attitudes," 357.

16. Heller and Johnson, "Parental Opinion," 555.

17. Splendorio and Reichel, *Tools for Teaching*, 97.

18. Ibid., 98.

19. Ibid., 99.

20. Ibid., 100.

21. Ibid., 102–103.

22. Ibid., 99.

23. Ibid., 98.

24. Zimmerman, *Too Hot to Handle*, 146.

25. Blair, "President Obama's Proposed Cuts."

26. Peruse, for instance, the popular Facebook page, "I fucking love science."

27. Halstead and Lewicka, "Should Homosexuality," 58.

28. Ibid., 59

29. Halstead, "Islam, Homophobia and Education," 40.

30. Halstead and Lewicka, "Should Homosexuality," 60.

31. Ibid., 52.

32. Ibid., 58.

33. Ibid., 62.

34. Merry, "Should Educators Accommodate Intolerance?"

35. Halstead, "Islam, Homophobia and Education," 37.

36. Ibid., 39.

37. Mohajir, *Starting the Conversation*, 2.

38. HEART Peers Program, *Let's Talk*, 3.

39. Ibid.

40. Zimmerman, *Too Hot to Handle*, 117.

41. Kendall, *The Sex Education Debates*, 1.

42. Ibid., 229.

43. Ibid., 236.

44. "National Sexuality Education Standards," 7.

45. Schmidt, Wandersman, and Hills, "Evidence-Based Sexuality," 188.

46. Zimmerman, *Too Hot to Handle*, 147.

47. Kendall, *The Sex Education Debates*, 61.

48. Wermund and Hefling, "Trump's Education Secretary."

Conclusion: Democracy, Education Standards, and Local Control

1. Klein, "1989 Education Summit."

2. Sparks, "Clarifying."

3. For which states presently use the Common Core, see "Map: Tracking the Common Core." See also Garland, "In Texas."

4. Rhodes, "Learning Citizenship?," 181–220.

5. Gamson, McDermott, and Reed, "Elementary and Secondary Education"; *Every Student Succeeds Act.*

6. Cohen and Moffitt, *Ordeal of Equality*, 141.

7. *Elementary and Secondary Education Act of 1965*, Section 604, p. 57.

8. Duncan, "Duncan Pushes Back."

9. Cited in Mehta, *Allure of Order*, 67.

10. *Elementary and Secondary Education Act of 1965*, Section 205, p. 31.

11. Cohen and Moffit, *Ordeal of Equality*, 81.

12. Ibid., 67.

13. See Mehta, *Allure of Order*, chapter 4.

14. National Commission on Excellence in Education, 113–130.

15. Mehta, *Allure of Order*, chapter 5.

16. Ibid., 222–223.

17. Gamson, et al., "Elementary and Secondary Education," 16.

18. *No Child Left Behind Act of 2001.*

19. Cohen and Moffit, *Ordeal of Equality*, 130.

20. US Department of Education, "ESSA."

21. Layton, "Senate Overwhelmingly Passes."

22. US Department of Education, "ESSA."

23. *Every Student Succeeds Act*; see also Alexander, "Every Student Succeeds."

24. *Every Student Succeeds Act*, 23.

25. Ibid.

26. Schwartz, "Every Student." The Common Core ELA anchor standards are also called "College and Career Readiness Anchor Standards for Language."

27. *Every Student Succeeds Act*, 20, 21.

28. McGuinn, "From No Child," 12–13.

29. Clukey, "In Spite of State Efforts."

30. The following paragraphs draw upon Schwartz, "Every Student."

31. *Every Student Succeeds Act*, 32.

32. Strauss, " 'Sit and Stare.' "

33. Office of Elementary and Secondary Education, Department of Education, "Final Regulations," 27.

34. *Revised State Template for the Consolidated State Plan.*

35. Klein, "Trump Education Dept."

36. Ujifusa, "Here's How."

37. Barnes, "Common Core"; Pullmann, "Yes, Donald Trump."

38. Darling-Hammond, Wilhoit, and Pittenger, "Accountability," 35.

39. Ibid., 6.

40. Ibid., 8.

41. Ibid., 8. Emphasis in original.

42. Ibid.

43. Ibid., 7.

44. Ibid., 13.

45. Ibid., 12.

46. Ibid., 5.

47. Ibid., 16, 8.

48. Ibid., 5. Emphasis added.

49. Ibid., 10.

50. Darling-Hammond, et al., "Accountability," 7.

51. Dewey, "The Classroom Teacher," 186.

52. Dewey, *The School and Society*, 37.

53. Ibid., 19.

54. Dewey, *Democracy and Education*, 197.

55. Lagemann, *An Elusive Science.*

56. Tampio, "In Praise of Dewey."

57. Ibid., 107.

58. Dewey, *Experience and Education*, 34.

59. Dewey, *Democracy and Education*, 102.

60. Ibid., 104.

61. Dewey, *The Public and Its Problems*, 156, 157.

62. Lipman, *The New Political Economy.*

63. Epstein, *A Different View*, 13.

64. Ibid., 40.

65. Ibid., 57.

66. Klein, "These Chicago Protesters."

67. Joseph, "Black Lives Matter"; Masterson, "Chicago Activists"; "Baltimore City Students."

68. Hagopian, "Six Reasons."

69. Gilens and Page, "Testing Theories," 564–581.

Epilogue: Democracy and the Test Refusal Movement

1. Chester E. Finn Jr. uses the verb "prune" to describe the Common Core's effect on the curriculum in his introduction to Gross, *Final Evaluation*.

2. E.g., Strauss, "Kindergarten Show Canceled."

3. Ravitch, "What's Not to Like."

4. *Race to the Top Program Executive Summary*.

5. See Sparks, "Clarifying."

6. Harris, "20% of New York"; Clukey, "In Spite of State Efforts." In the spring of 2017, over half of the eligible students on Long Island refused to take the state ELA exam; see "Opt-Outs."

7. The test refusal movement is strongest in the suburbs, in part because New York City's policy of using test scores to determine admission into middle and high schools makes it difficult for families to refuse the tests, and Title I schools need to be careful about contravening state education policies.

8. McGill, *Race to the Bottom*, 9.

9. Ibid., 3.

10. Zernike, "In High-Scoring Scarsdale."

11. McGill, *Race to the Bottom*, 26–37.

12. Ibid., 36.

13. Cited in ibid., 37.

14. Pizmony-Levy and Saraisky, *Who Opts Out and Why?*, 6.

15. Hynes, "Our Nation."

16. Hynes and Koerner, Interview.

17. Patchogue-Medford School District, "Road to Success."

18. Hynes, "Our Nation."

19. Burris, "How Many Students."

20. Bowman, Interview.

21. All of the quoted passages in this section are from Bowman, "Tyranny."

22. Campanile, "Principal Says."

23. On the image of a democratic public telling leadership whether a shoe fits or not, see Dewey, *The Public and Its Problems*, chapter 6.

24. "The CCSS is the latest, and most concerted, effort to use standards to leverage improvement across the American education system." Supovitz, et al., "The Bubble Bursts," 11.

25. Burris, "Embrace the Common Core."

26. Joy Pullmann raised this question on a Truth in American Education conference call on July 25, 2013.

References

Achieve. "How to Read the Next Generation Science Standards." Accessed January 23, 2017. https://www.youtube.com/watch?v=Q6eoRnrwL-A.

Alexander, Lamar. "The Every Student Succeeds Act and 'Common Core State Standards.'" Senate Committee on Health, Education, Labor & Pensions. 2015. https://www.help.senate.gov/imo/media/doc/ESSA %20-%20Ends%20federal%20Common%20Core%20mandate .pdf.

American Educator 14, no. 4 (Winter 2010–2011).

Arendt, Hannah. *The Human Condition*. Chicago: University of Chicago Press, 1998.

———. "Reflections on Little Rock." *Dissent* 6, no. 1 (1959): 45–56.

"Arguments against the Common Core." A Chicago Teachers Union Position Paper. July 2014. http://www.ctunet.com/quest-center /research/text/CTU-Common-Core-Position-Paper.pdf.

Ash, Katie. "Common Core Needs Tailoring for Gifted Learners, Advocates Say; Still, Educators May Have to Go Deeper to Meet the Needs of Such Students." *Education Week* 33, no. 10 (2013).

Ault, Charles R., Jr. *Challenging Science Standards: A Skeptical Critique of the Quest for Unity*. Lanham, MD: Rowman & Littlefield, 2015.

"Baltimore City Students Walk Out in Protest of the PARCC Test." *Baltimore Sun*. April 15, 2016. http://www.baltimoresun.com/news /86569271-132.html.

Barnes, Fred. "Common Core Has Disappeared from Trump's Remarks." *Weekly Standard*. March 1, 2017. http://www.weeklystandard.com /common-core-has-disappeared-from-trumps-remarks/article/2007024.

Barr, Elissa M., Eva S. Goldfarb, Susan Russell, Denise Seabert, Michele Wallen, and Kelly L. Wilson. "Improving Sexuality Education: The Development of Teacher-Preparation Standards." *Journal of School Health* 84, no. 6 (2014): 396–415.

Bartels, Lynn. "Jefferson County School Board Ridiculed on Twitter." *Denver Post.* September 23, 2014. http://www.denverpost.com/2014 /09/23/jefferson-county-school-board-ridiculed-on-twitter/.

Battista, Michael. "Research and Reform in Mathematics Education." In *The Great Curriculum Debate: How Should We Teach Reading and Math?*, edited by Tom Loveless, 42–84. Washington, DC: Brookings Institution Press, 2001.

Bauerlein, Mark. "A Concluded Battle in the Curriculum Wars." *Common Core Watch.* March 25, 2014. Accessed January 23, 2017. https:// edexcellence.net/commentary/education-gadfly-daily/common-core -watch/a-concluded-battle-in-the-curriculum-wars.

Beach, Richard, Amanda Haertling Thein, and Allen Webb. *Teaching to Exceed the English Language Arts Common Core State Standards: A Critical Inquiry Approach for 6–12 Classrooms.* 2nd ed. New York: Routledge, 2016.

Beals, Katharine, and Barry Garelick. "Explaining Your Math: Unnecessary at Best, Encumbering at Worst." *The Atlantic.* November 11, 2015.

Bindewald, Benjamin J., Rory P. Tannebaum, and Patrick Womac. "The Common Core and Democratic Education: Examining Potential Costs and Benefits to Public and Private Autonomy." *Democracy & Education* 24, no. 2 (2016): 1–10.

Blair, Leonardo. "President Obama's Proposed Cuts to Abstinence Education Are 'Indefensible,' Expert Says." *Christian Post.* February 22, 2016. http://www.christianpost.com/news/president-obama-cuts -abstinence-education-indefensible-valerie-huber-ascend-158364/.

Bowman, Jamaal. Interview with the author. January 18, 2017.

———. "The Tyranny of Standardized Testing." *Jamaal Bowman Word-press Blog.* August 31, 2015. https://jamaalabowman.wordpress.com /2015/08/31/the-tyranny-of-standardized-testing/.

Braun, Karen. "Good Grief! Charlie Brown Is 'College and Career Ready.'" *Stop Common Core in Michigan.* October 12, 2015. http://stopcommoncoreinmichigan.com/2015/10/good-grief-charlie -brown-common-core-standards/.

Burris, Carol. "Embrace the Common Core: IQ2 Debate." *IQ2*. September 9, 2014. https://www.youtube.com/watch?v=aYP_ORbahDo.

———. "How Many Students Are Refusing to Take Common Core Tests This Year?" *Washington Post*. April 6, 2016.

———. "View: New Math Pattern Doesn't Add Up." *Journal News*. July 26, 2014.

Campanile, Carl. "Principal Says Standardized Testing Is 'Modern-Day Slavery.'" *New York Post*. November 9, 2015.

Casey, Zachary A. "The Gettysburg Address in English Class: An 'Exemplar' of Common Core's Attack on Diverse Learners." *Journal of Curriculum Theorizing* 31, no. 1 (2016): 58–71.

Clukey, Keshia. "In Spite of State Efforts, Test Opt-Out Rates Remain High." *Politico*. July 29, 2016.

Cody, Anthony. "The Secret Sixty Prepare to Write Standards for 50 Million." *Education Week*. July 6, 2009.

Cohen, David K., and Susan L. Moffitt. *The Ordeal of Equality: Did Federal Regulation Fix the Schools?* Cambridge, MA: Harvard University Press, 2009.

Coleman, David. "Cultivating Wonder." New York, The College Board, 2013.

College Board. "Annual Results Reveal Largest and Most Diverse Group of Students Take PSAT/NMSQT®, SAT®, and AP®; Need to Improve Readiness Remains." September 3, 2015. https://www.collegeboard.org/releases/2015/annual-results-reveal-largest-most-diverse-group-students-take-psat-sat-ap.

———. "AP Course and Exam Description: AP United States History Including the Curriculum Framework: Updated Fall 2015."

———. "AP United States History 2016 Free-Response Questions."

———. "Reach Higher: Delivering on Common Core State Standards." 2012.

———. *Rubrics for AP Histories + Historical Thinking Skills*. 2015.

———. "SAT Practice Test #6." 2016.

———. "Statement on AP U.S. History." September 19, 2014. https://advancesinap.collegeboard.org/english-history-and-social-science/us-history/college-board-statement.

"Common Core State Standards English Language Arts." National Governors Association Center for Best Practices, Council of Chief

State School Officers. Washington, DC, 2010. http://www
.corestandards.org/ELA-Literacy/.

"Common Core State Standards for Mathematics." http://www
.corestandards.org/Math/.

"Conceptual Shifts." Michigan Association of Intermediate School
Administrators (MAISA). June 30, 2014. https://openaccess.kentisd
.org/Courses/3325/Units/4464/Lessons/6867.

Cowles, Henry. "Child's Play." *Aeon*. January 9, 2016.

Curry, Katherine A., Lou L. Sabina, and Jon Loffi. "Advanced Placement U.S. History and the Application of Social Justice." *Administrative Issues Journal* 6, no. 2 (2016): 30–52.

Danielson, Christopher. *Common Core Math for Parents for Dummies*.
Hoboken, NJ: Wiley, 2015.

Darling-Hammond, Linda. *The Flat World and Education: How America's Commitment to Equity Will Determine Our Future*. New York:
Teachers College Press, 2010.

Darling-Hammond, Linda, Gene Wilhoit, and Linda Pittenger.
"Accountability for College and Career Readiness: Developing a
New Paradigm." *Education Policy Analysis Archives* 22, no. 86
(2014): 1–38.

Darling-Hammond, Linda, Joy Ann Williamson, and Maria E. Hyler.
"Securing the Right to Learn: The Quest for an Empowering
Curriculum for African American Citizens." *Journal of Negro
Education* 76, no. 3 (2007): 281–296.

Decker, Geoff. "Algebra Pass Rates Fall amid Common Core Shift,
Leaving At-Risk Students Furthest Behind." *Chalkbeat*. November 5,
2015.

Dewey, John. "The Child and the Curriculum." In *John Dewey on
Education: Selected Writings*, edited by Reginald D. Archambault,
339–358. Chicago: University of Chicago Press, 1974.

———. "The Classroom Teacher." In *The Middle Works, 1899–1924*,
edited by Jo Ann Boydston. Vol. 15, 180–189. Carbondale: Southern
Illinois University Press, 1983.

———. *Democracy and Education*. In *The Middle Works, 1899–1924*,
edited by Jo Ann Boydston. Vol. 9. Carbondale: Southern Illinois
University Press, 2008.

———. *Experience and Education*. New York: Free Press, 2015.

———. "The Principle of Nationality." In *The Middle Works, 1899–1924*, edited by Jo Ann Boydston. Vol. 10, 285–291. Carbondale: Southern Illinois University Press, 1983.

———. *The Public and Its Problems: An Essay in Political Inquiry*, edited by Melvin L. Rogers. University Park: Pennsylvania State University Press, 2012.

———. *The School and Society & the Child and the Curriculum.* Lexington, KY: ReadaClassic, 2009.

Dudley, Renee. "College Board Faces Rocky Path After CEO Pushes New Vision for SAT." *Reuters.* December 12, 2016.

Duncan, Arne. "Duncan Pushes Back on Attacks on Common Core Standards." Arne Duncan Remarks at the American Society of News Editors Annual Convention, Capital Hilton, Washington, D.C. US Department of Education. June 25, 2013.

———. "Secretary Arne Duncan's Remarks at OECD's Release of the Program for International Student Assessment (PISA) 2009 Results." US Department of Education. December 7, 2010.

———. "Thinking beyond Silver Bullets." Remarks of Secretary Arne Duncan at the Building Blocks for Education: Whole System Reform Conference in Toronto. US Department of Education. September 13, 2010.

Eden, Max. *The Mend of History: A Study of the Revisions to the AP US History Framework.* Washington, DC: American Enterprise Institute, 2015.

Editorial Board. "Robert Small Deserves an Apology." *Baltimore Sun.* September 23, 2013.

Elementary and Secondary Education Act of 1965. Washington, DC: Government Printing Office.

Elkind, Peter. "Business Gets Schooled." *Fortune* 173, no. 1 (2016): 48–60.

EngageNY.org of the New York State Education Department. Accessed January 12, 2017. https://www.engageny.org/resource/grade-3-mathematics-module-5.

Epstein, Kitty Kelly. *A Different View of Urban Schools: Civil Rights, Critical Race Theory, and Unexplored Realities.* Rev. ed. New York: Peter Lang, 2012.

Every Student Succeeds Act. Washington, DC: Government Printing Office, 2015.

Feinstein, Noah Weeth, and Kathryn L. Kirchgasler. "Sustainability in Science Education? How the Next Generation Science Standards Approach Sustainability, and Why It Matters." *Science Education* 99, no. 1 (2015): 121–144.

Felton, Emmanuel. "How the Common Core Is Transforming the SAT." *The Atlantic.* October 29, 2015.

Fisher, Christine M., Susan K. Telljohann, James H. Price, Joseph A. Dake, and Tavis Glassman. "Perceptions of Elementary School Children's Parents regarding Sexuality Education." *American Journal of Sexuality Education* 10, no. 1 (2015): 1–20.

"Future of Sex Education Initiative." *National Sexuality Education Standards: Core Content and Skills, K–12* (a special publication of the *Journal of School Health*), 2012.

Gamson, David A., Kathryn A. McDermott, and Douglas S. Reed. "The Elementary and Secondary Education Act at Fifty: Aspirations, Effects, and Limitations." *RSF: The Russell Sage Foundation Journal of the Social Sciences* 1, no. 3 (2015): 1–29.

Garcia, Jefferson. "Jeffco Cancels Classes at Golden, Jefferson High Schools Due to Teacher Absences." *Chalkbeat.* September 24, 2014.

Garland, Sarah. "In Texas, New Math Standards Look a Whole Lot Like Common Core." *Hechinger Report.* May 26, 2016.

———. "The Man behind Common Core Math." *NPR: Blogs.* December 29, 2014.

Gewertz, Catherine. "Incoming College Board Head Wants SAT to Reflect Common Core." *Education Week.* May 6, 2012. http://www.edweek.org/ew/articles/2012/05/16/32collegeboard.h31.html?qs=gewertz+incoming.

Gilens, Martin, and Benjamin I. Page. "Testing Theories of American Politics: Elites, Interest Groups, and Average Citizens." *Perspectives on Politics* 12, no. 3 (2014): 564–581.

Goldstein, Dana. "The Schoolmaster." *The Atlantic.* October 2012.

Great Minds. "EngageNY Math Is Eureka Math." Accessed June 7, 2017. https://greatminds.org/math/eureka-is-engageny.

Gross, Paul R. *Final Evaluation of the Next Generation Science Standards.* Washington, DC: Thomas B. Fordham Institute, June 13, 2013.

Hagopian, Jesse. "Six Reasons Why the Opt Out Movement Is Good for Students and Parents of Color." *The Progressive.* March 19, 2016.

Haimson, Leonie. "Should You Trust a Computer to Grade Your Child's Writing on Common Core Tests?" *Washington Post.* May 5, 2016.

Halstead, J. Mark. "Islam, Homophobia and Education: A Reply to Michael Merry." *Journal of Moral Education* 34, no. 1 (2005): 37–42.

Halstead, J. Mark, and Katarzyna Lewicka. "Should Homosexuality Be Taught as an Acceptable Alternative Lifestyle? A Muslim Perspective." *Cambridge Journal of Education* 28, no. 1 (1998): 49–64.

Hamilton, Alexander, James Madison, and John Jay. *The Federalist Papers,* edited by Ian Shapiro. New Haven: Yale University Press, 2009.

Hamilton, Laura S., Brian M. Stecher, Julie A. Marsh, Jennifer Sloan McCombs, Abby Robyn, Jennifer Russell, Scott Naftel, Heather Barney, and RAND Education. *Standards-Based Accountability under No Child Left Behind: Experiences of Teachers and Administrators in Three States.* Santa Monica, CA: RAND Corporation, 2007.

Hanushek, Eric A., Paul E. Peterson, and Ludger Woessmann. *Endangering Prosperity: A Global View of the American School.* Washington, DC: Brookings Institution Press, 2013.

Harris, Douglas N., Helen F. Ladd, Marshall S. Smith, and Martin R. West. *A Principled Federal Role in PreK–12 Education.* Washington, DC: Brown Center on Education Policy at Brookings, December 7, 2016.

Harris, Elizabeth A. "20% of New York State Students Opted Out of Standardized Tests This Year." *New York Times.* August 12, 2015.

Hart, Beth, Elaine Carman, Danielle Luisier, Natasha Vasavada, and College Board. *Common Core State Standards Alignment: Advanced Placement.* New York: College Board, 2011.

Hauser, Debra, Monica Rodriguez, Elizabeth Schroeder, and Danene Sorace. "Education and the Path to a Sexually Healthy Nation." *Education Week* 31, no. 30 (2012).

Hayes, Nakonia. "How a War Hero Launched a War on Bad Math Instruction." *The Federalist.* August 15, 2016.

HEART Peers Program. *Let's Talk about SEX (Education): A Guide to Effective Programming for Muslim Youth.* HEART Women & Girls, 2014. http://heartwomenandgirls.org/wp-content/uploads/2014/01/HEART_Guide_sexed_programming.pdf/.

Heitin, Liana. "Approach to Fractions Seen as Key Shift in Standards." *Education Week* 34, no. 23 (2014).

———. "Eight Things to Know about the Science Standards." *Education Week* 35, no. 23 (2016).

———. "Free Teaching Website Expands on EngageNY's Mission." *Education Week* 35, no. 32 (2016).

———. "Here's What We Know about the Next Generation Science Standards Tests." *Education Week*. August 31, 2016.

———. "Next Generation Science Tests Slowly Take Shape." *Education Week* 36, no. 32 (2017).

———. "Updated Map: Which States Have Adopted the Next Generation Science Standards?" *Education Week*. August 31, 2015.

Heller, Janet R., and Helen L. Johnson. "Parental Opinion Concerning School Sexuality Education in a Culturally Diverse Population in the USA." *Sex Education* 13, no. 5 (2013): 548–559.

Henderson, Michael B., Paul E. Peterson, and Martin R. West. "The 2015 EdNext Poll on School Reform." *Education Next*, no. 1 (2016): 8–20.

Hernández, Javier C. "New Education Secretary Visits Brooklyn School." *New York Times*. February 19, 2009.

Hess, Frederick M., and Max Eden. "Surprise—the New AP U.S. History Framework Is Scrupulously Fair-Minded." *National Review*. July 30, 2015.

Howell, William G. "Results of President Obama's Race to the Top." *Education Next* 15, no. 4 (2015).

Hynes, Michael. "Our Nation May STILL Be 'at Risk.'" *Education Week*. January 6, 2015.

Hynes, Michael, and Lori Koerner. Interview with the author. April 3, 2017.

Joseph, George. "Black Lives Matter—at School, Too." *The Nation*. January 19, 2015.

Kane, Thomas J., Kerri A. Kerr, and Robert C. Pianta, eds. *Designing Teacher Evaluation Systems: New Guidance from the Measures of Effective Teaching Project*. Hoboken, NJ: Wiley, 2014.

Katz, Daniel. "Dear Common Core English Standards: Can We Talk?" *Daniel Katz, Ph.D.* (blog). September 19, 2014. https://danielskatz.net/2014/09/19/dear-common-core-english-standards-can-we-talk/.

Kendall, Nancy. *The Sex Education Debates*. Chicago: University of Chicago Press, 2012.

Klein, Alyson. "1989 Education Summit Casts Long Shadow." *Education Week* 34, no. 5 (2014).

———. "ESEA Reauthorization: The Every Student Succeeds Act Explained." *Education Week*. November 30, 2015.

———. "Trump Education Dept. Releases New ESSA Guidelines." *Education Week*. March 13, 2017.

Klein, Rebecca. "These Chicago Protesters Have Been Starving Themselves for 34 Days." *Huffington Post*. September 20, 2015.

Kurtz, Stanley. "APUSH Revisions Won't Do: College Board Needs Competition." *National Review*. July 30, 2015.

Lagemann, Ellen Condliffe. *An Elusive Science: The Troubling History of Education Research*. Chicago: University of Chicago Press, 2000.

Lasting Impact: A Business Leader's Playbook for Supporting America's Schools. Boston, MA: Harvard Business School, 2014.

Layton, Lyndsey. "How Bill Gates Pulled Off the Common Core Revolution." *Washington Post*. June 7, 2014.

———. "Senate Overwhelmingly Passes New National Education Legislation." *Washington Post*. December 9, 2015.

"Lead State Partners." *Next Generation Science Standards*. Accessed April 2, 2017. http://www.nextgenscience.org/lead-state-partners.

Levinson, Meira. "Democracy, Accountability, and Education." *Theory and Research in Education* 9, no. 2 (2011): 125–144.

Lewin, Tamar. "Backer of Common Core School Curriculum Is Chosen to Lead College Board." *New York Times*. May 12, 2012.

Lipman, Pauline. *The New Political Economy of Urban Education: Neoliberalism, Race, and the Right to the City*. New York: Taylor & Francis, 2012.

Masterson, Matt. "Chicago Activists Call for Action on Elected School Board Bill." *Chicago Tonight*. April 18, 2017.

McGill, Michael V. *Race to the Bottom: Corporate School Reform and the Future of Public Education*. New York: Teachers College Press, 2015.

McGuinn, Patrick. "From No Child Left Behind to the Every Student Succeeds Act: Federalism and the Education Legacy of the Obama Administration." *Publius: The Journal of Federalism* 46, no. 3 (2016): 392–415.

Mehta, Jal. *The Allure of Order: High Hopes, Dashed Expectations, and the Troubled Quest to Remake American Schooling*. New York: Oxford University Press, 2013.

———. "How Paradigms Create Politics: The Transformation of American Educational Policy, 1980–2001." *American Educational Research Journal* 50, no. 2 (2013): 285–324.

Meier, Deborah. *Will Standards Save Public Education?*, edited by Joshua Cohen and Joel Rogers. Boston: Beacon Press, 2000.

Merry, Michael S. "Should Educators Accommodate Intolerance? Mark Halstead, Homosexuality, and the Islamic Case." *Journal of Moral Education* 34, no. 1 (2005): 19–36.

Meyer, Heinz-Dieter. "Civil Society and Education—the Return of an Idea." In *Education between State, Markets, and Civil Society: Comparative Perspectives*, edited by Heinz-Dieter Meyer and William Lowe Boyd, 13–34. Mahwah, NJ: Taylor & Francis, 2001.

Milgram, R. James. "Review of Final Draft Core Standards." *Nonpartisan Education Review* 9, no. 3 (2013), 1–13.

Milgram, R. James, and Sandra Stotsky. *Can This Country Survive Common Core's College Readiness Level?* Fayetteville, AR: Department of Education Reform, University of Arkansas, 2013.

Miller, Edward, and Nancy Carlsson-Paige. "A Tough Critique of Common Core on Early Childhood Education." *Washington Post.* January 29, 2013.

Mohajir, Nadiah. *Starting the Conversation: Sexual Health Education for Muslim Youth*. HEART Women & Girls, 2014.

"More Teaching, Less Testing." Poster. New York State Allies for Public Education.

National Assessment Government Board. "Official Summary of Governing Board Actions." November 18–19, 2016.

National Association of Scholars. "Letter Opposing the 2014 APUSH Framework." June 2, 2015.

National Commission on Excellence in Education. "A Nation at Risk: The Imperative for Educational Reform." *Elementary School Journal* 84, no. 2 (1983): 113–130.

National Council for the Social Studies (NCSS). *College, Career & Civic Life C3 Framework for Social Studies State Standards*. Silver Spring, MD: NCSS, 2013.

National Research Council. *Developing Assessments for the Next Generation Science Standards*. Washington, DC: National Academies Press, 2014.

———. *A Framework for K–12 Science Education: Practices, Crosscutting Concepts, and Core Ideas*. Washington, DC: National Academies Press, 2012.

"National Sexuality Education Standards: Core Content and Skills, K–12." *American Journal of Health Education* 43, no. 1 (2012): 1–31.

New York State Education Department. "New York State P–12 Science Learning Standards, Kindergarten Topic: K. Forces and Interactions: Pushes and Pulls." Accessed January 23, 2017. http://www.p12.nysed .gov/ciai/mst/sci/documents/p-12-science-learning-standards.pdf.

———. "Race to the Top Application." Accessed June 20, 2017. https:// www2.ed.gov/programs/racetothetop/phase2-applications/new-york .pdf.

New York State Science Education Consortium. "Position Paper on Next Generation Science Standards." August 2013.

Next Generation Science Standards: Adoption and Implementation Workbook. Washington, DC: Achieve, 2013.

"Next Generation Science Standards: Appendix A—Conceptual Shifts in the Next Generation Science Standards." *NGSS Release*. April 2013.

"Next Generation Science Standards: Appendix C—College and Career Readiness." *NGSS Release*. April 2013.

"Next Generation Science Standards: Executive Summary." *NGSS Release*. June 2013.

Next Generation Science Standards: For States, By States. "Statement of Support." Accessed November 6, 2016. http://www.nextgenscience.org /sites/default/files/NGSS%20Business%20Support%20Letter%20 REVISED%206.25.14.pdf.

"Next Generation Task Portal." Accessed April 2, 2017. https://ngss -assessment.portal.concord.org/.

No Child Left Behind Act of 2001. Washington, DC: Government Printing Office, 2002.

OECD PISA. *PISA 2015 Released Field Trial Cognitive Items*.

———. "Sustainable Fish Farming." Accessed June 9, 2017. http://www. oecd.org/pisa/PISA2015Questions/platform/index.html?user=&domain =SCI&unit=S601-SustainableFishFarming&lang=eng-ZZZ.

Office of Elementary and Secondary Education, Department of Education. "Final Regulations." *Federal Register* 81, no. 236 (2016).

"Opt-Outs from Common Core Test on English 2017." *Newsday*. 2017.

Patchogue-Medford School District. "Road to Success: Bringing Life to Education: Plan for Years 2016–2021."

Pizmony-Levy, Oren, and Nancy Green Saraisky. *Who Opts Out and Why? Results from a National Survey of Opting Out of Standardized Tests*. Research Report. New York: Teachers College Columbia University, 2016.

Polikoff, Morgan S. "How Well Aligned Are Textbooks to the Common Core Standards in Mathematics?" *American Educational Research Journal* 52, no. 6 (2015): 1185–1211.

Pruitt, Stephen. "The Next Generation Science Standards: The Features and Challenges." *Journal of Science Teacher Education* 25, no. 2 (2014): 145–156.

Pullmann, Joy. "Yes, Donald Trump Can Repeal Common Core: Here's How." *The Federalist*. February 16, 2017.

Putnam Northern Westchester BOCES. *SCIENCE21: Science for the 21st Century: Manual for Administrators*. Rev. ed. 2008, 2009, 2011. Yorktown Heights, NY: PNW BOCES, 2005.

Race to the Top Program Executive Summary. Washington, DC: US Department of Education, 2009.

Ravitch, Diane. *The Death and Life of the Great American School System: How Testing and Choice Are Undermining Education*. Rev. ed. New York: Basic Books, 2016.

———. "The Fatal Flaw of the Common Core Standards." *Huffington Post*. May 24, 2014.

———. "Linda Darling-Hammond on the Common Core Standards." *Diane Ravitch's Blog*. October 24, 2013.

———. *National Standards in American Education: A Citizen's Guide*. Washington, DC: Brookings Institution Press, 1995.

———. "What's Not to Like about Exeter? Sidwell? Lakeside? Dalton?" *Diane Ravitch's Blog*. August 11, 2013.

———. "Why I Cannot Support the Common Core Standards." *Diane Ravitch's Blog*. February 26, 2013.

Reckhow, Sarah. *Follow the Money: How Foundation Dollars Change Public School Politics*. New York: Oxford University Press, 2013.

Revised State Template for the Consolidated State Plan. Washington, DC: US Department of Education, March 2017. https://www2.ed.gov /admins/lead/account/stateplan17/revisedstateplanfinal.pdf.

Rhodes, Jesse H. *An Education in Politics: The Origins and Evolution of No Child Left Behind.* Ithaca, NY: Cornell University Press, 2012.

———. "Learning Citizenship? How State Education Reforms Affect Parents' Political Attitudes and Behavior." *Political Behavior* 37, no. 1 (2015): 181–220.

———. "Progressive Policy Making in a Conservative Age? Civil Rights and the Politics of Federal Education Standards, Testing, and Accountability." *Perspectives on Politics* 9, no. 3 (2011): 519–544.

Robelen, Erik W. "Common Science Standards Make Formal Debut." *Education Week* 32, no. 28 (2013).

Robinson, Adam, John Katzman, and Staff of the Princeton Review. *Cracking the New Sat, 2016 Edition.* Natick, MA: Princeton Review, 2015.

Rogers, Melvin L. "Democracy, Elites and Power: John Dewey Reconsid-ered." *Contemporary Political Theory* 8, no. 1 (2009): 68–89.

Schmidt, Sara C., Abraham Wandersman, and Kimberly J. Hills. "Evidence-Based Sexuality Education Programs in Schools: Do They Align with the National Sexuality Education Standards?" *American Journal of Sexuality Education* 10, no. 2 (2015): 177–195.

Schneider, Jack. "Privilege, Equity, and the Advanced Placement Program: Tug of War." *Journal of Curriculum Studies* 41, no. 6 (2009): 813–831.

Schneider, Mercedes K. *Common Core Dilemma—Who Owns Our Schools?* New York: Teachers College Press, 2015.

Schoenfeld, Alan H. "The Math Wars." *Educational Policy* 18, no. 1 (2004): 253–286.

Schwartz, Ira. "Every Student Succeeds Act (ESSA) Orientation." Presented by Assistant Commissioner for Accountability, New York State Education Department, at Fordham University. October 24, 2016. www.p12.nysed.gov/accountability/ESSAOrientationWebinaro 91416Final.pptx.

Shah, Nirvi. "National Sexuality Standards Would Introduce Subject Early." *Education Week* 31, no. 17 (2012).

Simon, Stephanie. "Bill Gates Plugs Common Core." *Politico.* September 29, 2014.

Smith, Marshall S., and Jennifer O'Day. "Systemic School Reform."
  Journal of Education Policy 5, no. 5 (1990): 233–267.

Smith, Marshall S., Jennifer O'Day, and David K. Cohen. "National
  Curriculum, American Style: Can It Be Done? What Might It Look
  Like?" *American Educator* 14, no. 4 (1990): 10–17, 40–47.

"Snapshot: Tracking the Common Core." *Education Week* 36, no. 11
  (2016).

Sparks, Sarah D. "Clarifying Common Core." *Education Week* 36, no. 19
  (2017).

Splendorio, Dominick, and Lori Reichel. *Tools for Teaching Comprehensive
  Human Sexuality Education: Lessons, Activities, and Teaching
  Strategies Utilizing the National Sexuality Education Standards.*
  Hoboken, NJ: Wiley, 2014.

Spring, Joel. *Economization of Education: Human Capital, Global
  Corporations, Skills-Based Schooling.* New York: Routledge, 2015.

Staff of the Princeton Review. *Cracking the AP U.S. History Exam, 2017
  Edition: Proven Techniques to Help You Score a 5.* Natick, MA:
  Princeton Review, 2016.

Steadman, Mindy, Benjamin Crookston, Randy Page, and Cougar Hall.
  "Parental Attitudes regarding School-Based Sexuality Education in
  Utah." *American Journal of Sexuality Education* 9, no. 3 (2014):
  347–369.

Steiner, David, and David Coleman. *Bringing the Common Core to Life.*
  Albany: New York State Education Department, 2011.

Stern, Gary. "The New Math: 3 Concepts in 2 Years." *Journal News.*
  July 21, 2014.

———. "New York's School Reform Sidelined by Common Core."
  Journal News. May 10, 2014.

Strauss, Valerie. "College Board Bows to Critics, Revises AP U.S. History
  Course." *Washington Post.* July 31, 2015.

———. "Kindergarten Show Canceled So Kids Can Keep Studying to
  Become 'College and Career Ready.' Really." *Washington Post.*
  April 26, 2014.

———. "New Book: Obama's Education Department and Gates Foundation
  Were Closer Than You Thought." *Washington Post.* August 25, 2016.

———. "'Sit and Stare'—What Some Kids Who Opt Out of Tests Are
  Forced to Do." *Washington Post.* March 14, 2014.

Superville, Denisa R. "In Colorado School Board Recall, Money and Politics Drive Ouster." *Education Week*. 35, no. 12 (2015).

Supovitz, Jonathan A., Francine Stephens, Julie Kubelka, Patrick McGuinn, and Hannah Ingersoll. "The Bubble Bursts: The 2015 Opt-Out Movement in New Jersey." Working Paper. Consortium for Policy Research in Education, University of Pennsylvania, Philadelphia, 2016.

Tampio, Nicholas. "Democracy and National Education Standards." *Journal of Politics* 79, no. 1 (2017): 33–44.

———. "Do We Need a Common Core?" *Huffington Post*. May 7, 2012.

———. "In Praise of Dewey." *Aeon*. July 28, 2016.

Taylor, James M., and Joy Pullmann. "Heartland Institute Experts React to Release of Next Generation Science Standards." *The Heartland Institute: Freedom Rising*. April 10, 2013.

Tienken, Christopher. *Defying Standardization: Creating Curriculum for an Uncertain Future*. Lanham, MD: Rowman & Littlefield, 2016.

Tocqueville, Alexis de. *Democracy in America*, edited by Harvey Mansfield and Delba Winthrop. Chicago: University of Chicago Press, 2000.

Ujifusa, Andrew. "Here's How Some States' ESSA Plans Address Testing Opt-Outs." *Education Week*. April 5, 2017.

US Department of Education. "Every Student Succeeds Act (ESSA)." Accessed December 21, 2016. http://www.ed.gov/essa.

———. "More Than $28 Million in Grants Awarded to 42 States to Cover Fees Charged to Low-Income Students for Taking AP Tests." Press Release. August 27, 2013.

Vasquez Heilig, Julian, Heather Cole, and Angélica Aguilar. "From Dewey to No Child Left Behind: The Evolution and Devolution of Public Arts Education." *Arts Education Policy Review* 111, no. 4 (2010): 136–145.

Vinovskis, Maris A. "An Analysis of the Concept and Uses of Systemic Educational Reform." *American Educational Research Journal* 33, no. 1 (1996): 53–85.

Weiss, Joanne. "The Innovation Mismatch: 'Smart Capital' and Education Innovation." *Harvard Business Review*. March 31, 2011.

Wermund, Benjamin, and Kimberly Hefling. "Trump's Education Secretary Pick Supported Anti-Gay Causes." *Politico*. November 25, 2016.

What Does It Really Mean to Be College and Work Ready? Washington, DC: National Center on Education and the Economy, 2013.

Williams, Julie. "JW Proposal Board Committee for Curriculum Review." September 18, 2014. http://www.boarddocs.com/co/jeffco/Board.nsf /files/9NYRPF6DED70/$file/JW%20PROPOSAL%20Board%20 Committee%20for%20Curriculum%20Review.pdf.

Williams, Yohuru. "Rhythm and Bruise: How Cuts to Music and the Arts Hurt Kids and Communities." *Huffington Post.* September 17, 2014.

Winterhalter, Benjamin. "Computer Grading Will Destroy Our Schools." *Salon.* September 30, 2013.

Wood, Peter. "APUSH: The New, New, New History." *Academic Questions* 28 no. 2 (2015): 224–235.

Wu, Hung-Hsi. "Phoenix Rising: Bringing the Common Core State Mathematics Standards to Life." *American Educator* 35, no. 3 (2011): 3–13.

Wysession, Michael. W. "Next Generation Science Standards: Preparing Students for Careers in Energy-Related Fields." *The Leading Edge* 34, no. 10 (2015): 1166–1168, 1170, 1172–1176.

Yi, Keren. "College Board: Reconciling AP Exams with Common Core." *AASA.* February 23, 2013. http://www.aasa.org/content.aspx?id =27296.

Zernike, Kate. "In High-Scoring Scarsdale, a Revolt against State Tests." *New York Times.* April 13, 2001.

Zhao, Yong. *World Class Learners: Educating Creative and Entrepreneurial Students.* Thousand Oaks, CA: Corwin Press, 2012.

Zimba, Jason. "Critics' Math Doesn't Add Up." *Common Core Watch.* August 7, 2013.

———. "The Development and Design of the Common Core State Standards for Mathematics." *New England Journal of Public Policy* 26, no. 1 (2014): 1–11.

———. "When the Standard Algorithm is the Only Algorithm Taught." *Common Core Watch.* January 9, 2015.

Zimmerman, Jonathan. *Too Hot to Handle: A Global History of Sex Education.* Princeton, NJ: Princeton University Press, 2015.

Index

About the Author

Nicholas Tampio is an associate professor of political science at Fordham University. Tampio researches the history of political thought, contemporary political theory, and education policy. His first book, *Kantian Courage: Advancing the Enlightenment in Contemporary Political Theory*, considers how Anglo-American, Continental, and Islamic political theorists renovate Kant's critical philosophy. Tampio's second book, *Deleuze's Political Vision*, explains why Gilles Deleuze's masterpiece, *A Thousand Plateaus: Capitalism and Schizophrenia*, ought to enter the political theory canon. He began to research education policy after New York started to implement the Common Core in 2012. Tampio serves as an editor of *Politics and Religion* and writes for popular outlets such as *Aeon*, the *HuffPost*, and the *Journal News*. His work has been translated into Chinese, Hebrew, Italian, Japanese, Persian, Portuguese, and Turkish.